JANUA LINGUARUM

STUDIA MEMORIAE
NICOLAI VAN WIJK DEDICATA

edenda curat

C. H. VAN SCHOONEVELD

Indiana University

Series Minor, 135

LANGUAGE
IN THE PHILOSOPHY
OF HEGEL

by

DANIEL J. COOK

School of Liberal Arts
Brooklyn College
City University of New York

1973

MOUTON

THE HAGUE · PARIS

LIBRARY OF CONGRESS CATALOG CARD NUMBER: 72-94455

Printed in the Netherlands, by ZND, 's-Hertogenbosch

PREFACE

This book is an extensively revised version of a dissertation submitted in partial fulfillment of the requirements for a doctoral degree at Columbia University. Since it was written in the mid-sixties, the topic of Hegel and language has become a popular one in Germany. I have tried, especially in the Conclusion, to relate my work to the latest German scholarship. Given, however, the many schools and tendencies of Hegelian thought in Germany today, a detailed and lengthy *Auseinandersetzung* with scholarship on this topic would not be very illuminating to an English-speaking audience without adding several background chapters devoted to presenting these current trends – a task beyond the scope of this book.

I would like to thank the Heinrich-Hertz-Stiftung, sponsored by the Ministerium für Wissenschaft und Forschung of the German State of North-Rhein-Westphalia, for a grant which enabled me to do further research on Hegel at the University of Bonn and the Hegel Archives at the Ruhr University of Bochum. I am also grateful to the American Philosophical Society for a travel grant awarded in conjunction with the German grant. My final thanks go to Professor Josef Derbolav, Director of the *Institut für Erziehungswissenschaft* at the University of Bonn, for his help in enabling me to do research in Germany and in affording me the full use of the facilities of his Institute.

Parts of Chapter IV were originally published in *The Journal of the History of Philosophy* (April, 1972) as "Language and Consciousness in Hegel's Jena Writings".*

50548

This book is dedicated to my wife Lucille, without whom my work (and my life) might have been more efficient, but less rewarding.

DANIEL J. COOK
Bonn, 1972

TABLE OF CONTENTS

PART III
LANGUAGE AND ABSOLUTE SPIRIT

INTRODUCTION

Until the middle of the 18th century the problem of the nature and origin of language was not a central one for Western philosophy. Various philosophical theories concerning language were developed and discussed by many classical thinkers, but only in relation to a more central problem in epistemology or metaphysics.[1] Towards the end of that century, however, certain thinkers, especially in Germany, began to examine more closely the intellectual problems associated with language. Their interest was not solely anthropological or cross-cultural, but was motivated by the desire to shed light on the solution of certain recurrent philosophical problems.

The preoccupation with the problem of language and its role in man's intellectual development is viewed as having begun with J. G. Herder and the early Romantics and having culminated with Wilhelm von Humboldt.[2] More specifically, serious treatment of language as a distinctive intellectual category in German thought can be said to have begun with Herder's *Abhandlung über den Ursprung der Sprache*, written in 1772, and to have reached its climax with Humboldt's prefatory essay to his *Einleitung zum Kawiwerk*, composed in 1834.

[1] The best historical summary on this matter is the first chapter of Ernst Cassirer's *The Philosophy of Symbolic Forms*, tr. R. Manheim (New Haven: Yale University Press, 1953), I, 117-176, entitled "The Problem of Language in the History of Philosophy". Cassirer extrapolates various theories of language from most of the major philosophers since Plato, pointing out the relationship between such theories and the respective philosophies (empirical, rationalist, idealist) in which they are embedded.
[2] "[With Humboldt]... endet der Weg, den Herder begann, den die Romantik fortsetzte, und dessen Ziel die Erkenntnis des Geistes durch das Medium der Sprache war". E. Fiesel, *Die Sprachphilosophie der Deutschen Romantik* (Tübingen: J. C. B. Mohr [Paul Siebeck], 1927), 215.

The period from the early 1770's to the 1830's coincides with the life of G. W. F. Hegel (1770-1831). Although Hegel lived at a time when the problem of language was earnestly discussed, it is not treated systematically in his mature philosophical works. Yet if we examine Hegel's earlier writings, we soon discover that he devoted much thinking to the problem of language and its role in a philosophical system. My general purpose in this essay is to examine the work of Hegel, especially in his early period (up to his departure from Jena in 1807) in order to ascertain his conception of language and to better understand its role in his later "encyclopaedic" writings and Lectures. Such an approach will shed light on some of Hegel's methodological principles (especially in his *Phänomenologie des Geistes*) and counter-balance certain aspects of some of the contemporary interpretations of Hegel.

Hegel was the first German philosopher (and aside from Heidegger, perhaps the only one!) to take the problem of the relation of philosophy to natural language seriously; for him the nature and role of language is materially related to philosophy, and is not merely a formal question as to which terminology should be employed. To be sure, Hegel is also the first German philosopher who was greatly preoccupied with the related problem of how one should write philosophy. A further purpose of this essay is to show that Hegel's conception of the role of language *in* philosophy greatly influenced the manner in which he expressed his *own* philosophy.

The problem of philosophical terminology took on an added urgency for Hegel because of the growing desire to speculate in one's own national, natural language, rather than the more formal, philosophically technical languages of Latin or French. In wanting to be the first philosopher "to make philosophy speak German", Hegel was concerned with justifying this endeavor and reconciling it with any *particularistic* implications it might have for philosophy, whose goal had always been a system of thought with *universal* application and appeal.

This essay is divided into three main parts, each dealing with the role of language at one general stage of Hegel's system.

PART I

LANGUAGE AND INDIVIDUAL CONSCIOUSNESS

I

HEGEL ON THE STUDY OF LANGUAGES

A. STUTTGART AND TÜBINGEN: "UNDERSTANDING" AND THE STUDY OF THE CLASSICS

On New Year's Day, 1787, the following entry is found in Hegel's diary: "Mein Haupt-Augenmerk sind noch immer die Sprachen, und zwar wirklich die Griechische und Lateinische".[1] Hegel had an abiding interest in foreign languages, especially Greek and Latin, and translated many classical works as a student, including Longinus' *Treatise on the Sublime;* his diary at this time is full of entries in Latin. Already at the age of 16, as a student in the *Stuttgarter Gymnasium*, Hegel attempted to justify the importance of a close study of the classics, particularly through the exercise of translating excerpts from their original language into German. His earliest statement on this is called "Über das Exzipieren [sic]", found in his diary (March 1786).[2] He is specifically concerned with Latin and the charge that this procedure leads to a stilted and pompous *(schwülstiges)* style of writing, since the student, in his reading, is attracted to the quotable, but insubstantial "bon mot".

---

[1] *Dokumente zu Hegels Entwicklung*, ed. J. Hoffmeister (Stuttgart: Fr. Frommanns Verlag, 1936), 38.

[2] Hoffmeister gives a list of some of the works that Hegel must have read at the time and whose impact is unmistakable in his writings. No claim for originality in Hegel's thought is being made here, though his treatment of the material is revealing. The source most cited by Hoffmeister is Christian Garve (1742-1798), a popular German philosopher of the time. Both Hoffmeister (p. 444) and B. Teyssèdre, in his article "Hegel à Stuttgart", (*Revue Philosophique de la France et de l'Etranger*, CL [1960], 2, 217), quote lengthy passages from Garve showing the source – at times *verbatim* – of the young Hegel's thought.

Hegel concedes that this danger is not easily avoided.[3] Nevertheless the procedure is helpful in appreciating the peculiar strengths and qualities of a language in a fashion that philosophical study or ordinary usage cannot do. One learns to ponder the utter dissimilarity *(völlige Ungleichheit)* of German and other languages and it is primarily this fact that makes "Exzipieren" worthwhile. In what deeper way one gains by being acquainted with the peculiar fashion in which Greek or Latin, as opposed to German, expresses itself is not spelled out. In summary, all that one learns from this statement is that there are certain critical differences between languages and that one must avoid appropriating the superficial and bombastic when learning them, thus neglecting the natural and genuine.

Hegel's first philosophical justification for the study of foreign languages comes to light in an essay entitled "Über einige charakteristische Unterschiede der alten Dichter (von den neueren)" which is one of the last things he wrote before leaving Stuttgart. Taking up a theme common in his day, he states that we learn and use words and signs of ideas mechanically in our youth, but they remain lifeless and unappreciated until, through experience, we learn to think with them and manipulate them on our own. But even then our thinking is conditioned by the words we have previously learned and by the usual limitations, relations and usage they imply.[4] Only through the study of foreign languages do we learn to grasp and separate out universal concepts.[5]

While Garve and other thinkers of the day repeatedly discussed

[3]   "Denn man nimmt ganz allein und bloss auf die Worte und *Phrases* Rücksicht, gar nicht einmal auf den Geist, Natur usw. derselben, von Sachen ist gar nicht die Rede... [thus] das Natürliche und Echte der Sprache wird ganz vernachlässigt". Hoffmeister, *Dokumente*, 32.
[4]   "Erst nach und nach durch die Erfahrung lernen wir unsern Schatz kennen und etwas bei den Wörtern denken, die aber für uns schon gleichsam Formen sind, nach denen wir unsere Ideen modeln und welche bereits ihren bestimmten Umfang und Einschränkung haben und Beziehungen sind, nach denen wir alles zu sehen gewohnt sind". Hoffmeister, *Dokumente*, 50.
[5]   "Hierauf gründet sich, beiläufig zu sagen, ein Hauptvorteil, den die *Erlernung fremder Sprachen* hat, dass wir die Begriffe bald allgemein zusammenfassen, bald absondern lernen". Hoffmeister, *Dokumente*, 50.

Bewusstsein... ist daher nur Zeichen überhaupt...". The making of an object into a sign, into An-other-than-it-is-for-itself, is the crucial first step consciousness takes on the road towards objective Spirit and, finally, absolute knowledge. This attribution of meaning to various natural objects – and the concomitant recognition of the resultant change in consciousness' self-awareness – is the basis for Hegel's theory concerning the dialectical nature of experience as explicitly formulated in the Introduction to the *Phänomenologie des Geistes.*[29]

Hegel next traces the formation of a system of signs, a language, which goes beyond the natural, individual signs first created by consciousness. The meaning of the sign and its existence must now exist only for consciousness; consciousness must not have to depend upon a natural object – that has its own being for itself, its own *für sich sein* – for understanding the world about it and for communication. In other words, the sign as a natural, real object must disappear;[30] the medium for language must be sought elsewhere.

Hegel finds this medium in memory *(Gedächtnis)* or Mnemosyne, as the ancients called it. According to Hegel, the sense-intuition is made into something thought *(zu einem Gedachten)*, into an ideal spatio-temporal form that is other than the object which it originally perceived. This matter-of-memory *(Gedächtnissache)* – this name, as Hegel identifies it – is thus detached from its relation to the outside objective world and gains its own ideal existence through the activity of consciousness; it has its own being-for-itself, totally apart from the empirical world, and thus transcends and "does away" with physical objects used as signs.[31] By naming objects,

---

[29]   Diese *dialektische* Bewegung, welche das Bewußtsein an ihm selbst, sowohl an seinem Wissen als an seinem Gegenstände ausübt, *insofern ihm der neue wahre Gegenstand daraus entspringt,* ist eigentlich dasjenige, was *Erfahrung* genannt wird". *Phänomenologie des Geistes,* ed. J. Hoffmeister (Hamburg: F. Meiner, 1952), 73; G. W. F. Hegel, *The Phenomenology of Mind,* trans. J. B. Baillie (2d ed. rev.; London: Allen & Unwin, 1955), 142.
[30]   "das Zeichen als ein *Wirkliches* [muss] ebenso... verschwinden". *Jenenser Realphilosophie I,* 210-211.
[31]   "Im *Namen* ist sein empirischen *Sein,* dass es ein Konkretes in sich Mannig-

i.e., idealizing them, consciousness is better able to think about and manipulate them since such signs are not anchored in any specific natural object.

Though Hegel says that somehow names have their own being apart from the object or subject,[32] they are nevertheless ephemeral things. This ephemerality is acknowledged in Hegel's discussion of sounded tones *(tönend gegliederte Sprache)* – the existential medium of names. Such sounds are evanescent, ceasing to exist as soon as they are made. But it is just this ephemeral, free formlessness of sound which makes names particularly suited to serve as elements in the higher intellectual processes of abstraction and universalization.[33]

A name names an individual thing, but as a name, among many others, it has a non-individual relation to other names and categories within the medium of the memory of consciousness. A name expresses the definite, the concrete, but in doing so, at the same time, wrenches it out of its place in the spatio-temporal continuum and relates it to larger conceptual categories of the understanding. "Blue" not only refers to a specific color in a specific object, but is related to other colors, color in general and other concepts of the understanding in a way that it is no longer an individual, but a universal name.[34]

Hegel is at pains to point out that the individual object sensed does have a real existence, but that for the purpose of conceptualizing and understanding, when it is named it is raised out of this spatio-temporal continuum and necessarily seen as a nexus of various relations and universal concepts. The transcending of the individual object is a formal operation that does not undercut its ultimate reality; only the *claim* (and Hegel himself stresses this word) of

---

faltiges und Lebendes und Seiendes ist, aufgehoben, es zu einem schlechthin in sich einfachen Ideellen gemacht... Im Namen ist die *fürsich*seiende Realität des Zeichens vernichtet". *Jenenser Realphilosophie I*, 211.

[32] "Der Name aber ist an sich, *bleibend*, ohne das Ding und das Subjekt". *Jenenser Realphilosophie I*, 211.
[33] *Jenenser Realphilosophie I*, 211.
[34] *Jenenser Realphilosophie I*, 212-213.

being transcended is expressed in this process of naming, abstraction and universalization.[35]

In the "Jenenser Philosophie des Geistes (1805/06)",[36] Hegel deepens his conception of language and shows considerable originality. There is much less dependence upon artificial terminology and Hegel's thoughts flow more smoothly. What makes this draft difficult, however, is the change in emphasis and wording towards a freer, more ego-oriented system. Hegel's discussion on naming and language occurs almost at the outset of this draft and occupies a major part of the section on "subjective Spirit". The close relationship between the nature of language and the development of consciousness is never made more explicit in Hegel's writings.

Hegel begins this final unpublished draft by examining consciousness' emergence from the immediacy of the sensient, animal world. Consciousness first gains a sense of its own existence by making and internalizing *(Er-innern)* images *(Bilder)* of the objects it intuits, and then freely manipulating them.[37] This internal

---

[35] Since Hegel's position on this matter has been so seriously misunderstood, it might be best to quote the relevant passage in full. He says, "Die Einzelheit der Empfindung ist also durch diese Stufen zum bestimmten Begriffe gesteigert worden, dass sie in der empirischen Anschauung überhaupt als ein im Raume und der Zeit Seiendes gesetzt, ganz formal als ein Aufgehobenes gesetzt wurde, so dass es darin vollkommen für sich blieb, nur die *Forderung* des Aufgehobenwerdens an ihm ausgedrückt wurde". *Jenenser Realphilosophie I*, 213.

Hegel never denies the ultimate existence of individual objects of sensation. At the end of the second draft of his "Philosophy of Spirit", he states, "Insofern wir ihn [i.e., the sense object at hand] sehen, auch fühlen oder hören, sind wir es selbst, unmittelbar eins mit ihm [und mit ihm] erfüllt". *Jenenser Realphilosophie II*, 184.

[36] *Jenenser Realphilosophie II*, 177-273.

[37] *Jenenser Realphilosophie II*, 180-182. Hegel makes many puns throughout this draft. He displays several of his favorites, which reoccur frequently in his later thought. For example, the homonyms of *"meinen"* (to mean, suppose) and *"meine"* (what is mine or belongs to me). The connection between these two is developed at length in the *Phänomenologie des Geistes*, 86-88, and Paragraph 20 of the *Enzyklopädie*. Another pun used here is the one that likens what is his, *seine* (i.e. consciousness') to what is being, *Sein*. Hegel has a whole catalogue of such word-plays on various forms of the verb "to be". See also *infra*, Chapter VIII, Section A, "Speculative Elements in Ordinary Language".

world of images of external objects exists solely for the self, for me, or in Hegel's language, has *Fürmichsein*. The images become invested with another essence or meaning that is a function of the self and not the external object; it becomes a "wholly-other" *(ganzes Anderes)*, a sign. So far Hegel has retraced the process of representation and signification outlined in his first "Philosophie des Geistes".

In this draft, however, he gives a much larger role to the ego or self; Hegel now stresses this *"Fürmichsein"* of the object as sign, viewing it as an extension of the self. Thus the being of the object-sign is, in fact, the ego itself; the "I" itself posits itself or becomes an object to itself.[38] Hegel then traces the process of the externalization *(Ent-äussern)* of this existing inner world of signs (die selbst *da ist*), thereby endowing it with concrete existence *(Dasein)*.[39] It is consciousness' process of first internalizing and then externalizing images of the objects of the outside world, that characterizes the whole process of experience that occurs in the *Phänomenologie des Geistes*. In Hegel's words, an object's implicit, unrationalized being, its *ansichsein*, is made explicit and rational for the subject *(fürsichsein)* and then and only then can it attain actual concrete existence *(an-und fürsichsein)*, and its relations with and

[38] Hegel's phrases echo Fichte's notion of idealism quite strongly. Sentences like the following bear an unmistakable Fichtean imprint. "Ich setze mich besonders zum Gegenstände... sein [the sign's] Sein ist Ich selbst.... Das Ich ist hier als *Innres* des Dings selbst Gegenstand". *Jenenser Realphilosophie II*, 182.

The constant repetition of "Ich" in this draft leads one to suspect that Hegel came under the influence of Fichtean terminology, perhaps as an alternative to the Schellingian terms which he was gradually abandoning and whose abuse by others was severely condemned by him at this time. Though Hegel finally develops his own peculiar terminology, the effect of this turn towards a more ego-oriented, internalizing view of experience remains a vital element in his final system. Even here, however, Hegel retains a realistic side to his thinking, since he never doubts the independent existence of the object world and views the internalizing of the non-ego world as, in fact, set off by this very desire of consciousness to appropriate and make meaningful the brute, outside world.
[39] "Dies, dass Ich das Ding nur als Zeichen, sein Wesen aber als Ich, als Bedeutung, als Reflexion in sich anschaue, ist ebenso selbst *Gegen*stand, Innerlichkeit, die selbst *da ist*. Es ist *unmittelbare* Innerlichkeit, erst so; es muss auch ins Dasein treten, Gegenstand werden, umgekehrt [muss] diese Innerlichkeit äusserlich sein: Rückkehr zum *Sein*". *Jenenser Realphilosophie II*, 183.

effect *(wirken, Wirklichkeit)* upon the world about it be fully understood. Hegel begins in this draft to use terminology that later becomes an essential part of his method of philosophic explanation.

This critical step of giving concrete form and existence to the hitherto only internally rationalized images of objects is accomplished by the power of name-giving, by language ("die *Sprache* als die *namengebende Kraft*"). Language bestows an objective, determinate existence upon this subjective, internal world of signs. This power of language is the first working of *Geist* as *Geist*, for it creates an object (ein *Seiendes*) that is adequate to the concept or idea that consciousness has of it.[40] Language is the means whereby *Geist* first develops an external, rational form; it is, as Hegel later says in the *Phänomenologie*, the "*Dasein des Geistes*".

When we name an object, the first thing we do is to articulate *(aussprechen)* the *being* of the object. First of all, the object *is* "x" which is a name, a tone of my voice; this name is, like a sign, something quite other than the intuition of the object itself and, arbitrarily, a non-descriptive proper name. Upon hearing the name, e.g., lion (one of Hegel's favorite examples), we call up the appropriate sense image from our memory. It is this recreating of a previously seen image by a word that is the primal creative power which the human mind exercises. The imagined thought or object thus created and named subsists in a mental or spiritual *(geistige)* world with its own rational relations with various other named objects. The being *(Sein)* of such mental objects is determined by the network of categories and relations that man creates; it is his own *(sein, seinige)*.[41]

What Hegel is elucidating here is the transition from the remembered, imagined world of objects to a rational and categorized one, from a realm of images to a realm of names. It is in this critical transition from imagination to understanding that language

[40] *Jenenser Realphilosophie II*, 183.
[41] "Durch den Namen ist also der Gegenstand als *seiend* aus dem Ich herausgeboren. Dies ist die erste *Schöpfer*kraft, die der Geist ausübt.... Der Mensch spricht zu dem Dinge als dem *seinigen* und lebt in einer geistigen Natur, in seiner Welt, und dies ist das *Sein* des Gegenstandes". *Jenenser Philosophie II*, 183.

plays a central role. Through signification and naming, consciousness overcomes the initial opposition between itself and the outside world. By assigning names to empirical objects, consciousness effectively appropriates them as a means for expressing itself in the world. Inner ideas and feelings as well can now be externalized and communicated, consciousness thereby gaining a greater understanding of itself as well as its environment. The process of signification plays a critical role in the intellectual and social development *(Bildung)* of consciousness. Though consciousness gains a fuller sense of its own identity (viz., self-consciousness) through such practical activities as physical labor, interpersonal and intergroup conflict, these constitute more advanced forms of a dialectical process first adumbrated by Hegel in his treatment of signification and language.

A recent article by Jürgen Habermas[42] traces the origin of such notions as alienation *(Entfremdung)*, externalization or objectification *(Entäusserung)*, appropriation *(Aneignung)* and reconciliation *(Versöhnung)* to Hegel's Jena writings. Habermas is primarily interested in Hegel's ideas on alienation, labor, and personal interaction and shows how these concepts serve as models for understanding the development of Hegel's mature social, political and legal thought. In the light of our above discussion, it is interesting to note that Habermas, in his citations from the Jena writings, virtually skips over much of the material on language, assuming the primacy of *sittliche* interaction and mutual recognition.[43] This is evident even in the title of his essay, *"Arbeit und Interaktion"*. Habermas does acknowledge the importance of language for social interaction,[44] but nevertheless assimilates all stages of the "Philosophie des Geistes" to that of reciprocal

[42] "Arbeit und Interaktion: Bemerkungen zu Hegels Jenenser Philosophie des Geistes", *Natur und Geschichte: Karl Löwith zum 70. Geburtstag*, ed. H. Braun and M. Riedel (Stuttgart: Kohlhammer, 1967), 132-155.
[43] Marcuse can also be cited as an example of this approach, though he tends to stress the element of interpersonal conflict in these writings. *Reason and Revolution*, 74-77.
[44] "So ist Interaktion von eingelebten sprachlichen Kommunikationen abhängig". Habermas, "Arbeit und Interaktion", 145.

recognition.[45] Despite his neglect of the extensive material on signification and language, Habermas cannot avoid relying upon the mediation of language to characterize his thesis concerning the nature of *Geist*. In expounding upon the latter, he makes constant use of words such as "communicate", "communicative", "symbolic mediation", etc.[46]

The interest of most recent philosophers such as Habermas has been oriented toward those elements in Hegel's early thought which would explicate what Marx – as Habermas points out – lumped together as "*gesellschaftliche Praxis*". Marcuse and Kojève have also stressed the importance of labor and the struggle for recognition in their treatment of Hegel. In their desire to trace the origins and development of Hegel's social thought they have – unlike Marx, who at least dwelt on the theoretical origins of the *Bildungsprozess* and the notion of *Entfremdung* in his "1844 Economic and Philosophic Manuscripts", but then rejected Hegel's approach as insufficient and abstract – neglected the important role of such intellectual processes as signification and its subsequent development and systematization into a common universe of discourse. Marx and his disciples may have decided that Hegel's philosophy is meaningful only if it is "turned on its head", but that does not alter the fact that some of Hegel's earliest systematic thinking was greatly influenced by his understanding of the nature and role of language in the *Bildung* of consciousness.

[45] "die dialektischen Grundmuster der Darstellung und der Arbeit [können auch] mit der Dialektik des sittlichen Handelns auf *einen* Nenner gebracht werden. Denn dann kann das Verhältnis des namengebenden und des arbeitenden Subjektes zur Natur ebenfalls unter die Figur des gegenseitigen Anerkennens gebracht werden...". Habermas, "Arbeit und Interaktion", 148.
[46] Habermas, "Arbeit und Interaktion", 134, 135, 150, 153, *et passim*. To give one example: "Geist ist die Kommunikation Einzelner im Medium eines Allgemeinen, das sich wie die Grammatik einer Sprache zu den sprechenden oder wie ein System geltender Normen zu den handelnden Individuen verhält..." (135).

C. CONCLUSION

One facet of consciousness' experience upon being thrust out of its immediate natural condition was revealed in our first chapter. There Hegel dealt with this matter from a pedagogic viewpoint, stressing the nature of the learning process whereby we develop and apply the categories of understanding. The resultant estrangement of consciousness upon breaking out of its immediate world was one of the essential elements in the process. In this chapter we have examined the origin of the *Bildung* of consciousness. In explaining this other facet of the origin of understanding, we can see that the pedagogic need, so to speak, of separating oneself from oneself is based on the fact that consciousness' earliest experiences occur in such a fashion. This was made explicit by Hegel in the later draft of the "Philosophie des Geistes", where he says that "the I posits itself or becomes an object to itself". The study of foreign languages in effect recreates the conditions of man's first thinking processes; both can occur only when the initial immediacy of consciousness' experience is destroyed.

In this chapter, it has been shown that Hegel made repeated efforts to systematize certain ideas on language. Knowledge of these Jena-system drafts will enable us to understand Hegel's references to language in his mature thought. The paradox is that his *Jenenser Realphilosophie* elaborates considerably more on the role of language as a basic form of human expression than his later writings. In the *Enzyklopädie*, for example, the category of language is discussed under the heading of "Die Einbildungskraft", which in turn is part of the section entitled "Die Vorstellung". His explicit discussion of language, in § 459,[47] adds very little to what he already has said about language as the product of consciousness' sign-making activity in his Jena writings. In the *Phänomenologie des Geistes*, Hegel no longer views languages as an explicit level of expression in the development of consciousness, but rather as a means for understanding that very development. This change in the

---

[47]   *Enzyklopädie* (1830), 369-374; *Hegel's Philosophy of Mind*, 213-218.

role of language from a definite stage in his thought to a basis for explaining his thinking in general becomes apparent in the *Phäno-menologie*, to which we now turn.

III

LANGUAGE AND CONSCIOUSNESS IN THE
PHÄNOMENOLOGIE DES GEISTES

In his Jena "Philosophie des Geistes", Hegel argues that consciousness comes to terms with the world immediately confronting it only by progessively becoming aware of the essential mediating nature of human experience and knowledge. Consciousness attempts, however, to regain that immediacy which characterized its initial relation to the world, by signifying or naming objects, thus hoping to overcome its estrangement from them. But each time consciousness (or later, self-consciousness) attempts to order or master its world, theoretically or practically, the immediacy it anticipated is once again destroyed. This quest for true immediate knowledge – for a stable isomorphic relationship between consciousness' conception of its world and that world itself – is the theme of the *Phänomenologie des Geistes*. In this work, Hegel no longer uses the signifying activity of language as a first, explicit stage in the development of consciousness, but extends this linguistic dimension of experience to all levels of conscious existence. He often illustrates the dialectical nature of experience by analyzing the language used by consciousness to describe its particular *Weltanschauung*. Hegel views the dialectical process as immanent in the use of language itself; this was first seen in his treatment of the activity of signification in the later drafts of his Jena "Philosophie des Geistes".

Our purpose in the following chapters is to demonstrate that this relation between dialectic and language is assumed by Hegel's mature thought, even in situations or areas of human experience where its role is not explicitly dwelt upon. Hegel consistently attempted – especially in the "*existential*" situations of the *Phänomenologie* – to show that each stage of intellectual development, each determinate form of Spirit has a distinctive way of expressing itself. The nature and role of each distinct form of expression is characterized by the dialectical process of the experience which consciousness undergoes at each stage – theoretical, practical or social – at which it finds itself. In this chapter we shall examine the language of Consciousness *(Bewußtsein)*,[1] the first major section of the *Phänomenologie*. Hegel's repeated references to the words consciousness uses at its three stages of experience ("Sense-Certainty", "Perception", and "Understanding") will no longer appear fortuitous, since we know that from his earlier drafts of the "Philosophy of Spirit", Hegel regarded the expressive activity of language as a means for exhibiting the dialectical origins of knowledge.

A. HEGEL'S THREE ARGUMENTS AGAINST "SENSE-CERTAINTY"

Hegel begins his exposition in the *Phenomenologie* by describing that cognitive state which first occurs after crossing the threshold into conscious life. In this state that which confronts consciousness, or the Ego *(Ich)*, is apprehended immediately and unconditionally. This initial relation of immediacy between subject and object is called "sense-certainty" *(sinnliche Gewissheit)* by Hegel, for the ego is certain that what is immediately present to its senses represents the ultimate and essential truth that is to be known about the world. In his treatment of consciousness in "Sense-Certainty", Hegel dwells on the nature of this immediate relation between

---

[1] Three different uses of the word "consciousness *(Bewußtsein)*" should be distinguished. First, it is used to refer to the first major section of the *Phänomenologie des Geistes* where "the truth is for consciousness something other than itself". This use of the word shall be capitalized to distinguish it from the two following related uses. It refers to human consciousness in general as it undergoes development through Self-Consciousness, Reason and Spirit (these being the other three sections of the *Phänomenologie*, and hence also capitalized here). Finally, in this sense it will be used specifically (and often pejoratively) to refer to consciousness as it is described in Consciousness and parallel sections of other works of Hegel (e.g., the *Enzyklopädie*), often preceded by the word "natural" or "naive" – i.e., *"natürliche Bewußtsein"*.

subject and object and attempts to show that such a condition, when examined, is, in fact, a mediated one. His strategy is to show how natural (or naive) consciousness itself becomes aware of the mediated nature of its experience by demonstrating the dialectical nature of consciousness' own expression of its understanding of its sense-experience.

In the first argument of three arguments, Hegel portrays natural consciousness as beholding the object of its experience independent of any knowledge or meaning consciousness may have of it. The latter is presented as the simply immediate existent, the essential reality, the *object* (*Gegenstand* – that which stands over against, or simply confronts the subject). Hegel then undertakes to test this truth of sense-certainty: that the objects present to sense-experience immediately present themselves the way consciousness claims they do. In order to do so properly, however, Hegel believes that one must proceed to recreate the actual situation of this level of experience. He therefore undertakes a little *Gedankenexperiment:* naive consciousness in "sense-certainty" is asked, "What is the "This", the particular object which confronts consciousness?" Or reduced to its spatio-temporal elements, what is the "Now", what is the "Here"? If "Sense-Certainty" is correct, writing down, or preserving the true answer, e.g., "'Now' is night-time",[2] should not change anything. But later the "Now" *is not* night-time, but something else, noon-time. The "Now" as night is no longer something which *is*, but something which *is not*. The "Now" exists as something which is indifferent to the existence of any particular, immediate "Now" and in fact maintains itself through the negation and mediation of any specific "Now".

Such a simple entity, which exists through negation – to be neither this nor that, to be a *not-this [ein Nicht-dieses]*, and equally this as well as that – we call a *universal* [ein *Allgemeines]*. The universal is therefore in fact the truth of sense-certainty.[3]

---

[2] *Phänomenologie*, 81; Baillie, 151. Hegel plays on the words *"Wahrheit"* and *"aufbewahren"*, meaning "truth" and "to preserve" respectively.
[3] *Phänomenologie*, 82; Baillie, 152. Changes have usually been made in the Baillie translation wherever cited in this work.

The same thing happens if we take the other form of "This" for Hegel – the "Here". Consciousness in "Sense-Certainty" says, "'Here' is a tree". But if it turns around, the "Here" is no longer a tree, but something else, e.g., a house.

> The Here itself does not disappear, but remains in the disappearance of the house, tree and so on, and is indifferently house, tree. The This displays itself as *mediated simplicity*, or as *universality*.[4]

Thus the pure undetermined being first beheld by consciousness is indeed that but only in the mediated, abstract form of an empty universal and not in the immediate particular fashion which consciousness meant.

In the course of this argument, Hegel states that the dialectical experience which natural consciousness undergoes is present in the language it uses to describe its experience. The realization that the truth of the particulars of sense-experience is their universality, is a truth expressed in the language of natural consciousness. Words like "this", "here", and "now" do not express any particular characteristics of our experience, but rather are among the most general terms in the language. The language of "Sense-Certainty" is truer than its own immediate experience.[5] Consciousness' initial attempt at expressing its immediate experience makes it realize the dialectical quality present in its experience. What consciousness says refutes its own belief in immediate knowledge. The real truth of "Sense-Certainty" is expressed in the language it uses; the particulars of sense-experience can only be expressed as universals, because they can only be understood as universals.[6]

---

[4] *Phänomenologie*, 82; Baillie, 153.

[5] "Wir *stellen* uns dabei freilich nicht das allgemeine Diese oder das Sein überhaupt *vor*, aber wir *sprechen* das Allgemeine *aus;* oder wir sprechen schlechthin nicht, wie wir es in dieser sinnlichen Gewissheit *meinen*. Die Sprache aber ist, wie wir sehen, das Wahrhaftere; ..." *Phänomenologie*, 82; Baillie, 152.

[6] "in ihr [language] widerlegen wir selbst unmittelbar unsere *Meinung*, und da das Allgemeine das Wahre der sinnlichen Gewissheit ist und die Sprache nur dieses Wahre ausdrückt, so ist es gar nicht möglich, dass wir ein sinnliches Sein, das wir *meinen*, je sagen können". *Phänomenologie*, 82; Baillie, 152.

Hegel then turns to the other side of this argument against "Sense-Certainty", stressing not the "sense", but the "certainty". The meaning of the object experienced was determined, as we have seen above, by the knowing subject or consciousness. What allows one to say of any "This" that it *is* a "This" – a "Here" or a "Now" – is the presence of the subject rather than anything in the object. There is nothing in any particular object that tells us it is a "Here" or a "Now" for a knowing subject. So let us examine the claim to truth of consciousness in "Sense-Certainty" from the point of view of the subject or the ego.[7]

"Sense-Certainty" attends to the object in its ken, saying, "The Now is daytime because *I* see it". But it quickly realizes that another "I" can affirm a different thing to be the "Now" or the "Here". Both statements are true, yet one seems to cancel out the meaning of the other, leaving only the bare, universal "I" mediated through the negation of any particular things that any particular "I" happens to see. Consciousness in "Sense-Certainty" no doubt intends to refer to a particular conscious state of a specific consciousness, but once again is unable to say so. The inability of consciousness to refer to any one of its individual states – just as it could not refer to any one of the objects, the "thises" of its states – is an expression of the universal, non-particular quality of its experience.

Hegel's third and final argument against the belief of the ultimate truth of immediate knowledge as experienced by consciousness in "Sense-Certainty" is the longest and most carefully developed of the three arguments.[8] The claim to truth and certainty which

---

[7]   *Phänomenologie*, 82-83; Baillie, 152-153.

[8]   Theodore Bodammer, for example, neglects the special importance of this third argument, viewing it merely as an extension of the first two. "Auch das wortlose Aufzeigen schliesslich ist nur mehr eine Reaktion des sinnlichen Bewusstseins auf die Einsicht, dass es das, was ihm unmittelbar gewiss erschien, nicht auszusprechen vermochte". *Hegels Deutung der Sprache: Interpretationen zu Hegels Äusserungen über die Sprache* (Hamburg: F. Meiner, 1969), 81. Though Bodammer rightly claims that the dialectical process taking place in "Sense-Certainty" is not occasioned by language, he nevertheless appeals to some sort of "dialogue" between consciousness in "Sense-Certainty" and philosophical consciousness to explain the dialectical movement. If the im-

consciousness has put forth has thus far been disproven. But perhaps the experience of "Sense-Certainty" at this level of consciousness cannot be truly understood if one pole (the object) or the other (the "I") is analyzed. As Hegel says at the outset, the certainty of "Sense-Certainty" is "an immediate pure relation".[9]

The tension between the two poles of experience – the object and the subject – should be retained. Such a condition is most faithful to the actual experience of "Sense-Certainty". There is one "self-identical relation", where as yet there has been no differentiation between subject and object. This is the more fundamental sense-experience: *relation* itself is considered ultimate and immediate;

we have to put the *whole* of sense-certainty itself as its essence, and no longer merely one of its moments.... Thus it is only the *whole* sense-certainty itself which endures therein as *immediacy*, and consequently excludes from itself all opposition *[Entgegensetzung]* which previously had a place there.[10]

In this third argument consciousness cannot be forced into alternative situations so that it might observe the disparity between its own notion of truth as residing in the particulars of sensation and the experience it, in reality, undergoes. Furthermore, rather than *talk* about the objects of experience and be frustrated in our attempt to designate them individually, a non-linguistic gesture or activity, i.e., pointing, is relied upon. Hegel thus reverts to the immediate contextual situation itself: we shall

let ourselves *point* it *out*, for the truth of this immediate relation is the truth of *this* ego, which restricts itself to a *Now* or a *Here*. Were we to examine this truth *afterwards*, or stand *at a distance* from it, it would

---

manent, epistemological basis of Hegel's argument is not stressed – rather than its linguistic or "dialogical" aspect – then his position is susceptible to many of the attacks made upon it, beginning with Ludwig Feuerbach. Because of the long and still influential history of the latter's arguments against Hegel's treatment of sense-experience in "Sense-Certainty" in the *Phänomenologie*, a brief appendix to this work has been specifically devoted to Feuerbach's attack on Hegel.

[9] "die Gewissheit als Beziehung [ist] *unmittelbare* reine Beziehung". *Phänomenologie*, 80; Baillie, 150.

[10] *Phänomenologie*, 84; Baillie, 155.

have no meaning at all; for that would do away with the immediacy, which is of its essence.[11]

Even here, however, one is thrust *beyond* the cognition of the object; the evanescent nature of time does not allow us to alight upon one instant of that time. Also in space – as a "Here", *this* "Here" – the object "disappears" into the fabric of relations in which it is present in this one intuition. The individual object pointed out has a geographical position; it is present in a spatial medium, in a *beyond*. It is one "Here" among many "Here's". In merely pointing out the object, one places it in a continuum stretching from the "Here" of consciousness, through a plurality of "Here's", to the "Here" of the object.[12]

Thus an examination of this immediate state of sense-certainty yields the following analysis according to Hegel: rather than a parade of atomic "thises", each isolated and unrelated to the one before or after it (both temporally and spatially), we are confronted with an interrelated continuum of experience, with flux and movement. Hegel captures the tone of immediate experience, but claims that any *awareness* of it is not immediate, but mediated. Such mediation is not abstract or static, but represents the flow of concrete experience itself. Such experience is evidence that one must *go beyond* the particular itself in order to gain an understanding of it.

[The] very act of pointing out proves not to be immediate knowledge, but a process [Bewegung] from the Here 'meant' through a plurality of Heres to the simple Universal Here, which is a simple Universal Here, just as day is a simple plurality of Nows.[13]

In the last argument against the naive realism of "Sense-Certainty", Hegel explicitly avoids the use of language, of what is said *about* the individual objects of its experience, and resorts to the activity

---

[11] *Phänomenologie*, 85; Baillie, 156.
[12] *Phänomenologie*, 85-86; Baillie, 156-157.
[13] *Phänomenologie*, 86; Baillie, 157-158. It is interesting to note that such a key word as "*Bewegung*" is used by Hegel in this third argument and not in the previous ones.

the origin of a particular *Gedankensystem* in terms of words present in that particular culture, Hegel's emphasis on "universal concepts" is uncommon. This theme is a recurrent and developing one in his thought: the study of foreign languages enables us to grasp abstractions and universals more easily since they are not enmeshed in our everyday language and its concrete, but all-too familiar expression. The study of foreign languages is an excellent preparation for philosophy, since it helps us to think "universally", to become familiar with the abstract categories of understanding.

Though much of our language may be the result of arbitrary or contingent factors,[6] Hegel thought that there was one underlying rational structure which was expressed in all languages, though not equally well in each. In an essay, several months later,[7] Hegel elaborates upon this theme by stressing the differences in language and conceptual powers between the ancient Greeks and the Germans. Certain concepts, relations and ideas cannot be expressed in German because there is no appropriate word.[8] The lack of certain words in a language implies the lack of certain ideas and relational concepts.

The notion that the language of various cultures or peoples

[6] "Ein Teil der Sprache, die gemeiniglich unser erstes Studium ist, ist willkürlich, der andere philosophisch und beruht auf den Verhältnissen der Begriffe... er wird viele willkürliche Regeln der besondern Grammatik übertreten können: aber keine solchen, die in allen Sprachen Ungereimtheiten wären". Hoffmeister, *Dokumente*, 127.

[7] "Über einige Vorteile, welche uns die Lektüre der alten klassischen griechischen und römischen Schriftsteller gewährt", Hoffmeister, *Dokumente*, 169ff.

Hegel first articulates his view that the study of classical languages is the best propaedeutic to philosophy in this early piece of writing from his Tübinger-Zeit: "so sieht man, welch eine zweckmässige Vorbereitung zum Studium der Philosophie das Lesen derselben ist; man bringt dadurch doch schon einen Vorrat von abstrakten Begriffen, und eine wenigstens etwas geübte Denkkraft mit". Hoffmeister, *Dokumente*, 172.

Language is seen primarily as "Eine ganz begrenzte Sammlung bestimmter Begriffe, nach denen wir alles modeln, was wir sehen oder bemerken". Hoffmeister, *Dokumente*, 170.

[8] "dass sie [the Greek writers] überhaupt die Dinge in andern Verhältnissen ansahen, und diese Beziehungen aufeinander in ihrer Sprache ausdrückten, und also Begriffe hatten, die wir [nicht] haben können, weil uns die Worte dazu fehlen". Hoffmeister, *Dokumente*, 170.

(Völker) embodies certain ideas that others do not, and, therefore, that these foreign languages express things otherwise left unsaid was a common one at the time. Hegel is specifically concerned, however, with certain conceptual distinctions which are more clearly expressed in a classical language than in his native German. Through the study of ancient languages, the vague catagories of ordinary thinking will become more determinate *(an Bestimmtheit gewinnen)* and one's understanding thereby exercised and sharpened.

B. HEGEL'S SPEECH "ON CLASSICAL STUDIES"

The function of language study for Hegel is to help articulate the determinate categories necessary for understanding, which are usually only implicitly or vaguely present in our ordinary thinking and language. In a letter to his close friend Niethammer in 1812, Hegel even suggests that a knowledge of the classics may be the true introduction to philosophy, and that the study of philosophy itself is superfluous in Gymnasium studies.[9]

Many of Hegel's earlier ideas on the role of the study of classical languages and literature in intellectual development are brought together in a concentrated and incisive form in his speech as lector of the Nürnberg Gymnasium at the close of the school year, September 29, 1809.[10] Though his remarks here are pedagogically

---

[9] Hegel realizes that this is an odd claim for a professor of philosophy to make: "nämlich dass vielleicht aller philosophischer Unterricht: an Gymnasien überflussig scheinen könnte, dass das Studium der Alten das der Gymnasialjugend angemessenste und seiner *Substanz nach* die wahrhafte Einleitung in die Philosophie sei…". *Briefe von und an Hegel*, ed. Hoffmeister (Hamburg: F. Meiner, 1952), I, 418-419.

[10] "On Classical Studies", trans. R. Kroner. Appendix to *On Christianity*: *Early Theological Writings by Friedrich Hegel*, trans. T. M. Knox and intro. R. Kroner (New York: Harper & Bros., 1961), 330. Unless otherwise noted, the translations of Hegel's speech are Kroner's. The original text consulted is in *Hegels Nürnberger Schriften*, ed. J. Hoffmeister, Vol. XXI of *Hegel's Sämtliche Werke* (Leipzig: F. Meiner, 1938), 303-317. According to the program, this speech was simply called "Rede zum Gymnasial-Schuljahres-Abschluss am 29. IX. 1809"; the above title, "On Classical Studies", is the translator's.

oriented and have a pedantic air about them (which is under-standable, considering the circumstances under which they were given), Hegel does elaborate considerably upon this theme and relate it to the other features of his philosophy.

Hegel attempts to justify the need for continued study of the classics in their own languages, though many now deem them irrelevant and obsolete. The riches of ancient literature can only be enjoyed in their original language: "Their content can be approximately given us by translations, but not their form, not their ethereal soul".[11] Hegel's objection to translations is that in such copies, "the contrast between the content and the form that has not grown up with the content makes itself felt unmistakably".[12] This sundering of content from form, or *vice versa*, and the con-sequent danger of viewing one independently of the other is the basis of a recurrent warning in Hegel's thought. This possibility becomes acute when dealing with more complex intellectual matters and the means required for expressing them.

A second reason for the study of languages is their "grammatical study whose value cannot be too highly assessed, for it constitutes the beginning of logical training."[13] Even the mechanical study of the grammatical forms of foreign languages introduce one to the logical categories of understanding *(Verstand)*.

Grammar... has for its content the categories, the special products and concepts *[Bestimmungen]* of the understanding; in learning grammar, therefore, the understanding itself first becomes learned.[14]

Such studies enable one to make simple abstractions, the first step into the realm of the intellect.

Grammatical terminology teaches us how to move in the realm of abstractions. This study consequently can be looked on as a preliminary instruction in philosophy.[15]

[11] "On Classical Studies", 326.
[12] "On Classical Studies", 326.
[13] "On Classical Studies", 328.
[14] "On Classical Studies", 329.
[15] "On Classical Studies", 329.

The third and most profound reason for such linguistic studies originates from the mediated nature of a foreign language for its students.

In speaking our mother-tongue, unreflective habit leads us to speak grammatically; but with an ancient language it is otherwise and we have to keep in view the significance which the intellect has given to the parts of speech and call to our aid the rules of their combination.[16]

Only through the study of something which wrenches the young mind out of its immediate natural condition does true education, true culture *(Bildung)* begin.[17] The study of foreign languages is such a means; *Bildung* can begin only with the conscious confrontation of a subject with something initially alien to it. The latter must not be something "useful", or an object of immediate sense perception, according to Hegel, but rather something with intellectual content, which has value and interest in and for itself.

Hegel then elaborates upon the theory of learning implicit in his view of experience. Hegel claims that "we appropriate the world of antiquity not only to possess it, but even more to digest and transform it."[18] Such material must be made into an object for a subject: "the substance of Nature and Spirit must have confronted us, must have taken the shape of something alien to us, before it can become our object."[19]

Such a wrenching out of one's immediate world – such alienation *(Entfremdung)*, as Hegel calls it – is the condition of theoretical education or culture *(Bildung);* the imagination occupies itself

---

[16] "On Classical Studies", 330.
[17] "Since the categories of the understanding are present in us because we are intellectual beings *(Verstandesbestimmungen... verständige Wesen)*, and since we therefore understand them immediately, the first step in erudition *(Bildung)* consists in our really possessing them, i.e., in having made them the *objects* of our consciousness and having become capable of distinguishing them by means of characteristic marks" (Italics mine.). "On Classical Studies", 329.
[18] "On Classical Studies", 327.
[19] "On Classical Studies", 327.

with something non-immediate, something alien, something pertaining to recollection, to memory and to thinking.[20]

The need for separating consciousness from its natural, immediate condition so that its potential may be realized is filled by the remote world and languages of the classics. By appropriating such alien material we, so to speak, separate ourselves from ourselves: we gain the psychic distance necessary to become thinking, rational beings.

[20] "Für die Entfremdung, welche Bedingung der theoretischen Bildung ist, fordert diese... den leichtern Schmerz und Anstrengung der Vorstellung, sich mit einem Nicht-Unmittelbaren, einem Fremdartigen, mit etwas der Erinnerung, dem Gedächtnisse und dem Denken Angehörigen zu beschäftigen". *Nürnberger Schriften*, 312.

II

SIGNIFICATION: THE PRIMARY EXPRESSION OF CONSCIOUSNESS

Hegel thought that the study of classical languages and their grammar afforded the best way of exercising man's native reasoning powers. Such a discipline developed those qualities which consciousness required to understand the world about it. With this idea of the study of languages in mind, I should like now to examine Hegel's early thoughts on the nature of language in general and its role in the development *(Bildung)* of consciousness. The notion of signification and language present in some of Hegel's early writings constitute a primary source for understanding his theory of the dialectical nature of consciousness, especially as it is elaborated in the *Phänomenologie*. Whole sections of Hegel's early attempts at a systematic philosophy of Spirit deal with the role of signification and language in man's intellectual development.

A. EARLY SOURCES FOR HEGEL'S CONCEPTION OF LANGUAGE

Hegel's first comments on the nature of language are copied from 18th-century Enlightenment thinkers like Christian Garve (1742-1798) and A. G. Kästner (1719-1800). Both these popular German philosophers had felicitous or epigrammatic styles that probably appealed to the adolescent Hegel. Being a voracious reader whose interests led him almost anywhere, he read and copied excerpts from any books available to him, giving them his own very general headings, like "Philosophy", "Psychology", "Natural Theology" and "Investigation of the Faculties". One of these excerpts, running over twenty pages in Hoffmeister's *Documente zu Hegel's Ent-*

wicklung,[1] is of interest on several counts. It is the first piece dealing at length with psychology and the human faculties: many of Hegel's ideas concerning sensation, the imagination, memory and taste are present here. He eventually takes most of these notions over into his own general philosophy of subjective spirit, not changing their specific content as much as their respective positions, within his own system, in particular, his psychology.

Of more specific concern to us are Garve's remarks on the constitution of language and its origin out of a system of signs *(Zeichen)*. We initially learn a language (i.e., a system of signs and what they signify) mechanically and only later do we learn the generic implications, of which the words are only signs.[2] Language does supply us with a ready-made vocabulary whose real meanings can be understood only when the speaker is made aware of the ideas referred to. Unless the non-particular, categorial nature of such ideas and their interrelationships is made apparent, such words are not really understood.[3]

Yet the word "sign" *(Zeichen)* is used so often and in so many different ways, that it is difficult to understand exactly what *is* being signified. Is it a fleeting sensory impression, a concrete physical object, an image *(Bild)* of a perceived object or its representation *(Vorstellung)*, or finally the abstract concept or universal idea itself? Are these signs natural configurations of what they signify or mere conventions? Almost all writers at this time believed that language had its origin in signs and that these were signs of ideas, but the nature of the latter differ greatly among empiricist, rationalist, romantic and religious thinkers.[4]

---

[1] Pp. 115-136. Hoffmeister (*Ibid.*, p. 115) cites the source of this essay as "Garves Versuch über Prüfung der Fähigkeiten im VIII. Band der Neuen Bibl. der schönen Wissenschaften und freien Künste 1769".
[2] Hoffmeister, *Dokumente*, 122.
[3] Later Hegel calls such usage "abstract"; only when the categorial implications and their interconnections are understood can a word have concrete (i.e., universal) meaning. Hegel often distinguishes between conventional and philosophical meaning of common nouns by calling them "abstract" and "concrete universals" respectively.
[4] Thus a statement such as the following one is not specific enough: "Die

It is thus difficult to pinpoint the exact source of some of Hegel's earliest thoughts on language. The curious history of a fragment originally entitled by J. Hoffmeister "Hegels Erster Entwurf einer Philosophie des Subjektiven Geistes (Bern, 1796)" bears this out.[5] When Hoffmeister first discovered this manuscript, he thought it represented an early draft of a projected philosophy of subjective spirit. According to him, certain specific influences were obvious[6] and others generally apparent. Yet it was thought that this outline was a genuine, somewhat original work of Hegel's, written by him while he was house tutor in Bern.

Several years later, Hoffmeister, in his *Dokumente zu Hegels Entwicklung*, republished this so called "first draft", and titled it simply "Materialien zu einer Philosophie des subjektiven Geistes".[7] In his notes to this section,[8] Hoffmeister retracts many of his earlier statements concerning this early outline. He now places it in Hegel's Tübingen period, with influences possibly stemming even from his studies at Stuttgart, and claims that Hegel did not compose this outline, or even compile it. It was probably outline notes of lectures delivered by someone in the "Abel'sche Kreis" in Tübingen.[9]

Bedeutung einer selbstgeschaffenen Zeichensprache für die Fixierung der gedanklichen Gehalte ist von den Vertretern des Rationalismus in der philosophischen Methode Descartes, Hobbes, Locke, u.a. immer wieder betont". (J. Schwarz, *Hegels philosophische Entwicklung* [Frankfurt a/M: V. Klostermann, 1938], 340, n. 47.) To this list can be added Herder and even Hamann, so that such a general statement is not very helpful in pinpointing any particular influences or nuances. Cassirer gives an excellent summary of the various notions of language at this time, including the problem of what the signs of language were supposed to signify. *The Philosophy of Symbolic Forms*, I, 133ff.

[5]   *Logos*, XX, 2 (1931), 140-168.

[6]   For example, he makes a great deal of J. N. Tetens' *Philosophische Versuche über die menschliche Natur und ihre Entwicklung*, I, Vol. IV of *Neudrucke seltener philosophischer Werke*, Kant Gesellschaft edition (Berlin: Reuther & Reichard, 1913), citing its influence constantly throughout his edition of the outline. On its parts concerning language, J. G. Herder is cited and this influence will be discussed shortly.

[7]   Hoffmeister, *Dokumente*, 195-217.

[8]   Hoffmeister, *Dokumente*, 448ff.

[9]   Jakob Friedrich Abel (1751-1829) was professor of philosophy from 1772-1790 at the Karls-Schule in Stuttgart. Hegel had met him there and probably encountered him later at Tübingen, since Abel was called to the University

From this first outline, Hegel sketched and prepared many of his later thoughts on language. There is a deepening of the material and many changes are made in its final form in §§ 459-464 of the *Enzyklopädie,*[10] but most of the motifs, and even more revealing, almost all of the older terminology is retained. The best way to illustrate this is to examine briefly that very portion of the draft dealing with language, which is entered under the heading of "Verstand" or the "Vermögen der Begriffe" (Faculty of Concepts). As before, language is mentioned within the context of expressing and signifying universal representations and concepts. ("Begriffe [sind] allgemeine Vorstellungen".) Words are seen as signs, usually arbitrary, for these concepts, and the question asked is how understanding comes to these definite idea-signs.

We now come to the draft's explicit comments on language.[11] Two problems concerning the origin of language are examined: how does speaking originate (i.e., to which faculty can it be attributed) and how do our ideas become connected to their respective signs? With such a sketchy and fragmentary draft, on such a common 18th-century topic, it is difficult to pinpoint exact sources, but J. G. Herder's *Abhandlung über den Ursprung der Sprache* immediately comes to mind. Many of his ideas are present in the draft and several are mentioned by Hoffmeister: the notion of the origin of language out of certain natural tones and their causal connection – initially fortuitous, mechanical and arbitrary –

---

there in 1790. He is described as Schiller's favorite teacher in Stuttgart. Though Hegel may never have studied directly under Abel in either Stuttgart or Tübingen – since he was not teaching at the places Hegel attended in those respective cities – his influence upon the young student is marked. Hoffmeister traces many specific references – both in expression and overall structure – to Abel's work, *Über die Quellen der menschlichen Vorstellungen* (Stuttgart, 1786). He also downgrades Tetens' influence upon the text and mentions several other possible sources, especially such early commentators on Kant's first "Critique" as J. Schulze, in his work, *Erläuterungen über des Herrn Professor Kants Kritik der reinen Vernunft* (Königsberg, 1784).

10 G. W. F. Hegel, *Enzyklopädie der philosophischen Wissenschaften im Grundrisse* (1830), eds. F. Nicolin and O. Pöggeler (Hamburg: F. Meiner, 1959), 369-377.

11 Hoffmeister, *Dokumente*, 210-211.

with the "nichttönenden" objects.[12] These ideas were generally current and might not be specifically traceable to Herder,[13] but several distinctive elements would make Herder's essay a likely source: e.g., the use, in the outline, of "Blitz" (lightning) as a sign-word having a striking similarity to what it signifies, is one of Herder's most vivid examples.[14]

Other remarks are made that concern the superiority of an alphabet language over an hieroglyphic one and the advantages of a written, less-equivocal language over a spoken, nuance-filled one. These matters are examined at length in § 459 of the *Enzyklopädie*, where Hegel elaborates upon these themes and develops them into a criticism of Leibniz's goal of a universal language. Hegel's treatment of such topics differs from those current at the time in at least one crucial respect, whose probable source can be noted here. Hoffmeister, in commenting on this outline of notes, claims that Hegel ranks hearing above sight in his psychology, as opposed to others who wrote empirical psychology at the time (e.g., J. N. Tetens). Hoffmeister makes no mention of Herder when noting the primacy of hearing over sight and does not spell out the reasons for its preference by Hegel.[15] This is, however, a distinctive theme in Herder's *Abhandlung über den Ursprung der Sprache*.

Herder claims that since man comes to speech and invents language only through hearing, "hearing has in a certain sense come to be the middle one of the senses, the gateway to his soul, and the connecting link among the remaining senses.... The sense

[12] Hoffmeister, "Erster Entwurf...", 150.
[13] For example, J. G. Fichte, in an article cited by Hoffmeister, defines language as the *"expression of our thoughts through arbitrary signs"*. "Von der Sprachfähigkeit und dem Ursprung der Sprache", *Philosophisches Journal Einer Gesellschaft Teutscher Gelehrten*, I, 3 (1795), 256.
[14] J. G. Herder, "Essay on the Origin of Language", trans. A. Gode, *On the Origin of Language* (New York: F. Unger, 1966), 141-142. The German text is in *J. G. Herder: Sprachphilosophische Schriften*, ed. E. Heintel (Hamburg: F. Meiner, 1960), 3-87.
[15] Thus he says, "Interessant ist dabei, dass Hegel (im Gegensatz zu Tetens) das Gehör im Rang höher stellt als das Gesicht. (Gesicht und Gehör verhalten sich ja wie Verstand und Vernunft.)", Hoffmeister, "Erster Entwurf...", 150.

for language has become our central and unifying sense;..."[16]
Herder argues that the superiority of the sense of hearing arises out
of its mediating role with the rest of the senses. Hearing promises
the possibility of communication because it combines and mediates
the signs of various feelings and visions that in themselves are
either too obscure or refined and complex. Hearing is also the most
vivacious *(lebhaft)* of the senses: "Touch overwhelms; vision is
too cold and aloof. The former cuts into us too deeply to be
qualified for becoming language; the latter remains too quiet
before us".[17] Hearing alone combines clarity with vivacity.

Furthermore, hearing is the most temporally-oriented sense for
Herder, most capable of capturing and reproducing, through
language, the flux of human experience. In stressing the dynamic
aspect of language, Herder distinguishes himself from his contemporaries. Hegel adopted this view of language in a passage
which is found in what Karl Rosenkranz called "Fragmente
historischer Studien"[18] and entered by Hoffmeister under the
material from Hegel's *Hauslehrerjahre* in Frankfurt. This fragment
(like many of the others of this period) was inspired by his reading
of Greek literature and history and concerns the mourning women
mentioned by Thucydides during the first year of the Pelopon-
nesian War. Hegel begins by talking of the need for alleviating
pain by crying out and thus "objectifying" it. Pain, though utterly
subjective, is projected out, thus benefitting the mourners and
preventing them from being engulfed in their own despair. This
release can occur only through oral means, not visual ones. Pictures
and eidetic images are static; talk *(Rede)*, however, is the best
form for objectifying what is otherwise subjective. Talk (or any
oral expression) is not yet objective, but nevertheless the motion
towards objectivity.[19] Language has a way of dynamically re-

---

16   "Essay on the Origin of Language", 142-143.
17   "Essay on the Origin of Language", 144.
18   *G. W. F. Hegels Leben* (Berlin: Duncker & Humblott, 1844), 515-532.
19   "Ein Gemälde tut diese Wirkung nicht. Er [sic] sieht nur, aber bewegt sich
nicht selbst. Die Rede ist die reinste Form von Objektivität für das Subjektive.
Sie ist noch nichts Objectives, aber doch die Bewegung nach Objektivität".

presenting that movement towards objectification so necessary for mediating between ourselves and what lies beyond us.

Furthermore, Herder sees the products of hearing and speaking, a language or ordered system of signs, as the external expression of man's reasoning powers:

Thus language appears as a natural organ of reason, a sense of the human soul, as the power of vision – in the story of the sensitive soul of the Ancients – built for itself the eye and the instinct of the bee builds its cell.[20]

Hegel also develops this notion of language as the most immediate expression *(Dasein)* of man's rationality in his Jena writings and uses it there in reconstructing the development of various forms of rational expression and human institutions. In fact, the reflective, ordered articulation and institutionalization of man's experience – the movement towards objectification as Hegel calls it – best expresses what he means by "Spirit" *(Geist)*. The rational reconstruction of the development of such a process is that part of a *Realphilosophie* which Hegel, in his Jena writings, calls a "Philosophie des Geistes". We now turn to the relevant sections of the so-called "Jena-Systems" in order to examine the primary role of signification and language for the *Bildung* of consciousness.

B. SIGNIFICATION AND LANGUAGE IN HEGEL'S "JENA-SYSTEMS"

In considering the three "Jena-systems",[21] which Hegel wrote while he was an instructor at the University there, special care must

---

Hoffmeister, *Dokumente*, 262. The importance of crying and articulated language in mourning is discussed by Hegel in the Zusatz to §401 of the *Enzyklopädie*. G. W. F. Hegel, *System der Philosophie. Dritter Teil. Die Philosophie des Geistes*, Vol. X of *Sämtliche Werke*, ed. H. Glockner (Stuttgart: Fr. Frommanns, 1929), 146; *Hegel's Philosophy of Mind*, trans. W. Wallace together with the *Zusätze*, trans. A. V. Miller with Foreword by J. N. Findlay (Oxford: Oxford University Press, 1971), 87.
[20] "Essay on the Origin of Language", 128.
[21] I refer here specifically to the following texts: "System der Sittlichkeit",

be taken. Like the material considered thus far, these systems were not meant for publication. In utilizing them for our purposes, we have to be aware that Hegel's thought here is present in a rudimentary, as well as fragmentary, form. The editors of these systems (most likely lecture notes from the courses Hegel taught at Jena) had to classify the material, insert titles for portions of it and add words occasionally to make sense out of certain passages. Hegel crossed out, rewrote and reworked sections so often that the continuity of his thoughts is sometimes impaired. Though he philosophizes here more systematically than previously, one cannot approach these drafts with the idea of finding a satisfying order or conclusion to his thoughts. One might object to calling these unpublished Jena drafts "systems", but the use of such a term is justified if it is taken as describing the fact that these writings do have an over-all architectonic, employing certain levels and categories of explanation (e.g., language, labor, national spirit, etc.). Though his system in these drafts is not fully developed, a definite pattern is followed, showing that Hegel did make attempts at organizing certain ideas he had concerning language.

The first of these drafts, the "System der Sittlichkeit", is probably the most obscure; it has been called "one of the most difficult in German philosophy".[22] Hegel uses words like *"Potenz"*, *"Differenz"* and *"Subsumption"* in a strange and artificial fashion. Such terminology has obviously been taken over, most likely from

---

Hegels Schriften zur Politik und Rechtsphilosophie, ed. G. Lasson (Leipzig: F. Meiner, 1913), 419-503; "Philosophie des Geistes", *Jenenser Realphilosophie I: Die Vorlesungen von 1803/1804*, ed. J. Hoffmeister (Leipzig: F. Meiner, 1932), 195-241; "Jenenser Philosophie des Geistes", *Jenenser Realphilosophie II: Die Vorlesungen von 1805/1806*, ed. J. Hoffmeister (Leipzig: F. Meiner, 1931), 179-273. The titles of the latter two works as well as the names of the above sections are Hoffmeister's; the second of these has been recently reprinted but re-entitled *Jenaer Realphilosophie: Vorlesungsmanuskripte zur Philosophie der Natur und des Geistes von 1805-1806* (Hamburg: F. Meiner, 1967). For the latest and most detailed chronology of Hegel's Jena-writings, see H. Kimmerle, "Zur Chronologie von Hegel's Jenaer Schriften", *Hegel Studien*, IV (1967), 125-176.
[22] Herbert Marcuse, *Reason and Revolution: Hegel and the Rise of Social Theory* (Boston: Beacon, 1960), 56.

Schelling, and Hegel is not "at home" in it. He begins this draft by tracing the relation of an individual to the world that surrounds him and the means or media (labor, children, talk) required to appropriate that world for his own needs; of interest to us is the last or most rational means, talk *(Rede)*, and more specifically its highest form, *tönende Rede.*[23]

Hegel is not discussing fully developed spoken languages, but rather elementary, even primitive forms of expression. Such a broad conception of language was common among German Romantics at this time. After mentioning the fleeting sound or gesture *(Gebärde)* and the corporeal sign *(körperliches Zeichen)*, Hegel ends by discussing sounding speech *(tönende Rede)* as the medium of intelligence. With this type of expression, the totality of internal feelings and ideas immediately find a definite, articulate, individualized form. It is this idea of speech as the most rational means *(Mitte)* for conveying one's internal feelings in some sort of individually characterized totality that should be noted here.[24]

In Hegel's first "Philosophie des Geistes (1803/04)"[25] we have a much more systematic approach to a "Philosophy of Spirit". There is still a large, unassimilable residue of the terminology that was present in the *System der Sittlichkeit.* Memory, and its product language, for example, are referred to as the first potency *(Erste Potenz)*. Nevertheless, much more is said about language, especially its crucial role as the primary medium *(Mitte)* for the development of individual consciousness and its social integration.

Hegel begins this draft[26] by discussing the first or "formal" existence of mind or spirit: consciousness *(Bewusstsein)*. Consciousness at this point refers to a sort of primitive awareness that

23   *Hegels Schriften zur Politik und Rechtsphilosophie,* 433-435.
24   *Hegels Schriften,* 435-436.
25   *Jenenser Realphilosophie I,* 195-241.
26   H. Kimmerle claims that much of the material in this draft was worked in later by Hegel but nevertheless concludes: that "Eine kurze, gedrängte Darstellung der drei Potenzen der 'formale Existenz' des Bewusstseins... [ist] als ältester Kern der Fragmente zu einer 'Philosophie des Geistes' zu betrachten". *Das Problem der Abgeschlossenheit des Denkens,* Supplement 8: *Hegel Studien* (Bonn: Bouvier, 1970), 248.

remains undifferentiated from its community. Such a consciousness becomes aware of its own individuality first through language, for by speaking, it separates itself from the other opposed consciousnesses to whom it speaks. Several pages later Hegel begins in earnest an exposition of his views on signification, naming and language.

Hegel first discusses the problem of signification within the context of consciousness' attempt to appropriate the objects in the world about it for its own self or, in Hegel's words, "to overcome completely the opposition of subject and object".[27] Unable to do this practically, consciousness does it theoretically: it ascribes to that which is contemplated *(Angeschautes)* an ideal meaning or existence which transcends its position in the objective world in which it remains located. (At this point we are talking of a dumb consciousness *[stummes Bewusstsein]* so that spoken or written signs are not yet at issue.) This ideal dimension is what Hegel calls a sign, *Zeichen*. He is intent upon emphasizing certain aspects in this process of signification. This sign, or ideal meaning, has an existence above and beyond both the significator, consciousness, and that which is signified, but this depends upon the meaning which consciousness confers on the object. The signs themselves do not explain or necessarily reflect this process of signification, since signs are arbitrarily assigned to objects by the subject. Thus the *meaning* of the sign – i.e., its ideal subsistence (and not the object's own existence or its being-for-itself, its *Fürsichsein*) – exists only in relation to the subject and is understandable only through it and for it.

According to Hegel, it is of the very nature of an object in our natural world to exist or subsist as a sign for a subject as well as to exist for itself *(für sich)*. The process of signification of natural objects is defined as its being posited as An-other-than-it-is-for-itself, something other than its natural meaning and existence (its *Fürsichsein*). Objects in the natural world are designated by sub-

---

[27] In Hegel's words "den Gegensatz des Subjekts und Objekts vollkommen aufzuheben...". *Jenenser Realphilosophie I*, 210.

jective consciousness as signs signifying something determined by the subject itself. Such signs have a natural existence that is not forgotten; they are not purely conventional signs, deriving their actual physical existence and *raison d'être only* from the meaning attributed to them by the imagination of the conscious subject. Such pure signs or names constitute a more developed form of signification, which Hegel discusses later.[28]

What makes Hegel's analysis so difficult is that he gives no concrete examples or specific illustrations of such prelinguistic signs. Furthermore, his ideas on this point are not developed in his later thinking on signs in § 458 of the *Enzyklopädie*, so that one cannot be certain to what he is referring. It would seem that natural physical objects to which ideal (non-natural) meanings are attributed are what Hegel is talking about. Such things as trees, snakes and eggs might qualify. Certain natural properties or configurations are taken over and used by consciousness when it invents its "sign language"; it is for this reason that Hegel concludes this section by stating that the sign-object "does not have its absolute meaning in itself, that is, Nature (viz., its natural properties) is not transcended in it", as it would be with a purely conventional language sign, a name, made up of letters in the alphabet or mathematical symbols.

Sign-making is the first expression of consciousness' attempt to overcome its alienation from the world about it. The very nature of consciousness is characterized by its sign-making activity ("Das

---

[28] Hegel's own words should be quoted to appreciate how difficult his prose is in the *Jenenser Realphilosophie* and to show how he uses many of the terms mentioned in our exposition. "Das Bewusstsein... ist daher nur *Zeichen* überhaupt, worin ein Angeschautes, als ein aus seinem Zusammenhänge Gerissenes, als auf ein Andres bezogen gesetzt wird, aber ideell, dass es noch in Wahrheit in seinem Zusammenhänge besteht; die Bezeichnung ist seine ausser ihm seiende Idealität und diese ist selbst ein Bestehendes, *ein Ding*, unendlich darin, das aber eine andere Bedeutung hat, als es ist, gesetzt als ein Anderes, als es für sich ist, zufällig für das, dessen Zeichen es ist, für sich nicht mehr es selbst seiend... die Bedeutung des Zeichens ist nur in Beziehung auf das Subjekt; es hängt von seiner Willkür ab, und [es] ist nur durch das Subjekt selbst begreiflich, was dieses sich dabei denkt; es hat nicht seine absolute Bedeutung in ihm selbst, d.h., die N[atur] ist in ihm nicht aufgehoben". *Jenenser Realphilosophie I*, 210.

of pointing, which should be more capable of isolating and referring to such sense-particulars. But Hegel then proceeds to show that even the dumb activity of pointing is subject to the same dialectical process which the experience of naive consciousness undergoes through its use of language. Thus the dialectical process of experience, while immanent in the language of "Sense-Certainty", and best understood philosophically *(für uns)* through an analysis of such language, is not to be thought of as resident solely in that language, but in sense-experience itself. One's inability to denote specifically such sense-particulars is not simply the fault of language, but reflects the nature of the conscious universalizing process of knowledge itself. The limitations of language are the limitations of understanding itself. It is impossible for someone to say what he means because the sense-particular which is referred to is inaccessible to language since language, as the inherently universal, simply expresses the knowing activity of consciousness itself.[14]

Consciousness in "Sense-Certainty" cannot say what it means because it really does not know what it means; its failure to verbalize its meaning is the failure of its knowledge, not its language. It is important that Hegel's argument be clearly understood, because many have faulted him for it. For example, J. Loewenberg attacks Hegel's argument in "Sense-Certainty" as based upon "the false hypothesis that the incommunicable can be represented as if it were communicable." Naive consciousness' inability to express itself "proves only the inadequacy of our modes of expression..." The contradictions in sense-certainty in which Hegel glories are "not *in* sense-certainty, but only *between* it and speech."[15]

[14] "Wenn sie wirklich diese Stück Papier, das sie meinen, sagen wollten, und sie wollten *sagen*, so ist dies unmöglich, weil das sinnliche Diese, das gemeint wird, der Sprache, die dem Bewusstsein, dem an sich Allgemeinen angehört, *unerreichbar* ist". *Phänomenologie*, 88; Baillie, 159.
[15] *Hegel's "Phenomenology": Dialogues on The Life of Mind* (La Salle, Illinois: Open Court, 1965), 39. Lowenberg's earlier formulation of this position is found in his article, "The Comedy of Immediacy in Hegel's 'Phenomenology'", *Mind*, XLIV (1935), 21-38.
Other commentators on Hegel have made the same point, but none have argued it as forcefully as Loewenberg. For other critical analyses of Hegel's argument in "Sense-Certainty", see C. Andler, "Le fondement du savoir dans

Loewenberg's argument is based upon the premise that not only is language "alien to sense-certainty," but any form of expression will distort the experience of naive consciousness.[16] But Hegel's point is that while such enjoyment certainly does exist, it can make no cognitive claims; it is a state of prerational *aesthesis* whose experience is strictly private, transient and incorrigible. When Loewenberg says that "He who silently enjoys the sensible qualities of things cannot be charged with contradiction unless he stoops to argue",[17] Hegel would reply that he can't be charged with *anything* since such ineffable feelings of enjoyment cannot be the basis of *any* coherent claims about the nature of reality.[18] Language, by its very nature, does conspire with the experience of sense-certainty to cancel out any notion of a particular individual object of knowledge, but this conspiracy is not the fault of the *words* consciousness uses to express itself. It should be remembered that Hegel is not saying that *because* such sense-particulars are ineffable, they don't really exist. Hegel does not deny the existence of such particulars, nor the authenticity of the intuition which beholds them. What he is saying is that the existence of these particulars is immediately and constantly transcended, not only in the linguistic process of denoting, but in our very experience of them as objects always present in relation to other objects beyond them.[19] One is justified

la Phénoménologie de l'Esprit", *Revue de Metaphysique et de Morale*, XXXVIII (July-September, 1931), 317-340; C. Nink, *Kommentar zu der grundlegenden Abschnitten von Hegels Phänomenologie* (Regensburg: 1931), 20ff. W. Purpus, in *Die Dialektik der sinnlichen Gewissheit bei Hegel* (Nurnberg, 1905), traces this argument back to the classic Skeptical tradition.

[16]   The "enjoyment of sense-certainty is one thing, expression of it quite another". Loewenberg, *Dialogues*, 36.

[17]   Loewenberg, *Dialogues*, 39.

[18]   In this sense, I think Hegel would agree with Croce's comment about the beginning of the *Phänomenologie*. "But the sensible certainty, of which Hegel speaks, is not the first theoretic form; it is not genuine sensible certainty, *aesthesis* pure and simple. It is not, as he believes, immediate consciousness: it is already mingled with intellectual reflection, it already contains the question as to what is truly real". B. Croce, *What is Alive and What is Dead in Hegel's Philosophy*, trans. D. Ainslie (London: Macmillan Co., 1915), 122.

[19]   Further light is shed on this relationship between consciousness and the universalizing nature of language in the one specific place in Hegel's *Jenenser*

in viewing this non-individual context or field of the particulars of sense-experience as a universal, as Hegel does. This does not conform to the usual abstract notion of universal, but rather to a more dynamic process.

What makes Hegel's arguments unpalatable to many are his references to over-arching universals which seem to negate the very being of the particulars of sense-experience. J. N. Findlay, for example, says that "Hegel is wrong in supposing that the word 'I' has some covertly universal meaning".[20] Later he says that "the mere fact that the pronoun 'I' can be used to refer to different persons, and implies no fixed set of properties, does not mean that it stands for something mystically common to various persons".[21] This typically English mistrust of some mysterious metaphysical universal is understandable. Yet sandwiched in between these two remarks, Findlay supplies part of the meaning that Hegel himself attributed to universals.

The pronoun 'I' together with expressions like 'you', 'it', 'this', 'here', 'now', etc., belongs to a class of expressions which may be called 'referential', and 'contextual'. Their function is to refer to, to pick out some definite object, either contained in the immediate situation or recently referred to, and to do so without by their use implying what *sort* of object is being referred to – *except perhaps in certain general respects* [italics in this last phrase are mine] – and further to be tied up with a particular 'referent' (or object referred to) by the *context* in which they are used, so that we cannot determine *what* thing is referred to *apart* from this context, and so that the same expression may refer to *different* things in different contexts.[22]

Realphilosophie I where he discusses the role of language *per se*, rather than that of naming, signification, etc. He sees language as the existential, external form of consciousness ("der existierende Begriff des Bewusstseins"); it embodies in its manifold of names, an ideal counterpart to the objects and relations beheld by consciousness. Language, as the "voice of consciousness" articulates and brings out the non-individual relations or universal elements of the isolated names. In thus ideally reflecting the common denominator and relationship of various named objects, language is in fact a form of understanding, that faculty which groups and judges things according to various categories. *Jenenser Realphilosophie. I* 211-212.
[20]   *Hegel: A Re-examination* (New York, N. Y.: Collier, 1962), 50.
[21]   Findlay, *Hegel*, 50-51.
[22]   Findlay, *Hegel*, 50.

Hegel is in perfect agreement with the sentiments of this citation. One important feature of such demonstratives is that they betray certain "contextual" situations and relations, and they do so *at all times, universally*. This "mystical" or "covertly universal" meaning of demonstratives nothing other than this awareness of the contextual element *always* present when such words are used. Hegel's whole point is that the naive consciousness of "Sense-Certainty" says nothing *about* the objects of its experience, but indeed only *refers* to them, thinking, however, it is saying something *about them* in particular, about their own intrinsic nature or qualities.

One thing that Hegel means when he uses the term "universal", is precisely this contextual element, the indispensable "beyond" of any sense-experience. In the impossibility of wrenching anything out of its total fabric of existence in order to know it "in itself," Hegel finds the empirical basis for a belief in the existence of certain non-individual entities and relations, or, as he prefers to call them, universals. Although one may question the exact nature of this notion of universals, as opposed to our ordinary understanding of them, Hegel does effectively refute the idea that individual sense-particulars are epistemologically ultimate. He demonstrates how such a view is superseded by one which regards objects not so much as "things" "meant" and simply pointed out, but, more truthfully and scientifically, as points of attachment for universals, as various focal points in a field of experience: a philosophy of perception may call these universals qualities or spatio-temporal relations. Furthermore, Hegel believed that the usage of universals (such as demonstratives) as specific indicators pointed to a dialectical quality resident in experience was worth examining philosophically.

Language is the first means whereby these universals, implicitly present in our non-linguistic perception and experience, are explicated and expressed. The various categories adumbrated dialectically by Hegel from experience are present in language; he ironically describes this as the "divine nature" of language which transmutes the particular into the universal. However, even if language is not used, the result is the same.

If I want, however, to help out speech – which has the divine nature of turning the mere 'meaning' right round about, of making it into something else, and so of not letting it really be expressed in words at all – by pointing out this bit of paper, then I get the experience of what is, in point of fact, the real truth of sense-certainty. I point it out as a Here, which is a Here of other Heres, or is in itself simple many Heres together, i.e., is a universal.[23]

Hegel shows that such words as "I", "This", "Now", and "Here" prefigure the truth of the immediate experience consciousness undergoes. He also makes this same point by playing on the literal meanings – of which consciousness is not immediately aware – of the words it uses. For example, Hegel concludes the section on "Sense-Certainty" by playing on the German word for perception, "*Wahrnehmen*" (literally, to take truly). The assumed immediacy of sensation, when understood, enables consciousness to take or apprehend the nature of the objects of its experience as in truth they are: nexi for the universal qualities perceived by consciousness.[24]

B. THE LANGUAGES OF PERCEPTION AND EXPLANATION

The section immediately following that of "Sense-Certainty" in the *Phänomenologie* is called by Hegel "Perception or Thing and Deceptiveness" ("Die Wahrnehmung; oder das Ding und die Täuschung"). Consciousness in perception is aware of the mediated nature of the objects present to it; it views what it sees as a *thing with many properties*, a "*This*" that is in effect a nexus of many "not-Thises" or universals. It says that these *different* universals or properties co-exist in the *same* thing, compatible with, but indifferent to, one another: "we say of the thing, 'it is white, and *also* cubical, and *also* tart', and so on". The word "also" refers to the *thing* as

---

[23] *Phänomenologie*, 88-89; Baillie, 160.
[24] "ich nehme so es [the sense-particular] auf, wie es in Wahrheit ist, und statt ein Unmittelbares zu wissen, *nehme ich wahr*". *Phänomenologie*, 89; Baillie, 160.

"the general medium wherein the many properties subsist externally to one another, ... without cancelling one another".[25]

But, according to Hegel, each property has a reality and exclusive identity apart from and beyond its presence in this particular object with its own characteristic set of properties: we say *"so far as* it is white it is not cubical, and *in so far as* it is cubical and also white it is not tart, and so on".[26] Consciousness then realizes that it can reconcile the apparent contradiction present in perception (viz., how the necessary *simplicity* of a thing can be compatible with the *diversity* of its properties), only by positing the existence of an underlying *unperceived* substance or substratum. The need for such a doctrine is brought to light through the language *perceiving* consciousness has to use to come to terms with its world. The language of perception thus carries with it its own dialectical undoing; the language of "Here" and "Now" in "Sense-Certainty", which became the language of "Also" and "in so far as" in "Perception" in turn becomes the language of general scientific laws in "Understanding".

In "Force and Understanding: Appearance and The Supersensible World" ("Kraft und Verstand: Erscheinung und übersinnliche Welt"), as the final part in Consciousness is called, Hegel deals with the critical transition from consciousness to self-consciousness. His involved discussion has many fascinating aspects, but we shall highlight only one point: the role of language in initial attempts at scientific explanation. The experience and language of consciousness in "Perception" made it realize the need for a non-perceptual, intelligible framework in order to understand its world. Such a supersensible framework – whether governed by doctrines concerning substance or laws of nature – is endowed by consciousness with the power of explaining the sensible world. Yet a general law such as that of the universal attraction of bodies is articulated in so pure and generalized a form that it transcends all the particular phenomena it was meant to explain. Nevertheless,

---

[25] *Phänomenologie*, 96; Baillie, 171.
[26] *Phänomenologie*, 96; Baillie, 171.

consciousness is at least brought to realize the importance of giving expression to this bare conception of a law in order to give some meaning to what otherwise is a parade of accidental particulars.

The Understanding thinks it has found a universal law [i.e., the law of the universal attraction of bodies] which expresses general reality *as such*. Yet it has in fact only discovered the *conception* of *law itself*, but nevertheless in such a fashion that it at the same time declares: *all* reality *in itself* conforms to law. The expression of *universal attraction* thus has great import in so far as it is directed against unthinking representation [Vorstellen], to which everything is presented in the pattern of contingency and in the form of independent sensuous existence.[27]

Consciousness soon realizes, however, that though the elements necessary for explanation (i.e., the general concepts and particular constructs of metaphysical or scientific theories) are alternately separated and united in thought, they are not distinguishable or present *as such* in reality. Therefore, such general explanations are strictly verbal and tautological in the sense that they merely repeat the same idea in different words.[28] Such a process of explanation would seem unnecessary, but it does serve the purpose of making consciousness (in "Understanding") aware that the manner in which it attempts to come to terms with the world really involves coming to terms with itself. The constructs and concepts which consciousness in "Understanding" utilizes are projections of its own intellectual requirements. When consciousness realizes that the supersensible world discovered through the process of explanation is a world of its own creation, it becomes self-consciousness: "consciousness of self in its otherness [i.e., the external world]". Such a realization occurs through the agency of language which is the means for the articulation of such general laws of nature.

Thus it can be shown that at all three stages of Consciousness – "Sense-Certainty", "Perception" and "Understanding" – language plays a significant role in the way consciousness comes to terms with its world. Furthermore, the dialectical process of experience

27   *Phänomenologie*, 116; Baillie, 196-197.
28   *Phänomenologie*, 119-120; Baillie, 200-201.

that Hegel outlines in the *Phänomenologie* appears to be immanent in the language consciousness itself uses to describe its world. As we have just seen, Hegel often analyzes these various languages to illustrate the dialectical movement underway.[29]

[29] T. Bodammer discusses the relevant passages on language in the first two sections in Consciousness and claims that the role of language in these sections is characteristic of its role in later stages of consciousness in the *Phänomenologie*. However, he claims that the appearance of language is only occasional. Furthermore, he develops no thesis concerning the relationship between language and consciousness in the *Phänomenologie*, other than to state simply that the "given-ness" (*Vorgegebenheit*) of language in the *Phänomenologie* enables Hegel to reflect upon various levels of consciousness and indicate their particular ways of expression. *Hegels Deutung der Sprache*, 86-87.

PART II

LANGUAGE AND COLLECTIVE CONSCIOUSNESS

IV

REASON, LANGUAGE AND THE SPIRIT OF A PEOPLE

In the first chapters the relation of individual consciousness to the reality that immediately confronted it was examined. The role of language for Hegel in revealing the dialectical nature of experience to consciousness was demonstrated. Thus far, only the relationship of individual consciousness to language has been discussed; little has been said of the relation of a people *(Volk)*, or society in general, to the world it confronts and the nature and role of language in such a confrontation. In order to understand the transition from the experience of individual consciousness to that of social or national consciousness, it is necessary to trace Hegel's ideas on the specific manner in which a people *(Volk)* expresses its collective experience. In this chapter we shall deal primarily with Hegel's early views, before the *Phänomenologie*, on the relation between a collective group and its language. The stage of Reason *(Vernunft)* in Hegel's thought in general and the *Phänomenologie* in particular can be actualized only on the level of an organic community of consciousnesses,viz., a civil society or a state.

If our thesis is correct, this critical dialectical transition from Understanding to Reason, from individual consciousness (Consciousness and Self-Consciousness) to the collective experience of a people (Reason and Spirit), will be expressed in the character and role of the language used by the individual consciousness undergoing this transformation.

For Hegel, the development of both history and philosophy occurs through the progressive realization of ideal categories and institutions possible only in an organized society or people. Just as certain modes of expression reflect certain levels of individual consciousness, so certain kinds of language betray the intellectual and spiritual categories of a people or society. Throughout the early part of his philosophical career Hegel displayed a strong interest in this relationship between the spirit of a people *(Volks-geist)* and the language it used. It is in this connection that Hegel, in his Jena-period writings, makes his most forceful presentation on the need for developing a native, German terminology adequate to expressing the deepest philosophic matters. The spirit of the German people, according to Hegel, can only be fully realized when it is able to philosophize in its own tongue. Hegel's statements in his later writings on the need for a proper language for philosophy are grounded upon his earlier experiences in his quest for a German language adequate to expressing his own thoughts.

A. BERN AND FRANKFURT: LANGUAGE AND "VOLKSGEIST"

In 1793, Hegel finished his studies at Tübingen and became a family tutor in Bern, Switzerland. In looking over Hegel's literary products during his *Hauslehrerjahre* (three in Bern and then three in Frankfurt), one notices immediately a change in the direction, temper and content of his thought. Whether it be the reaction of a young Swabian to the deadening life of the aristocracy in Bern, the aftermath of the excitement over the French Revolution, or, most likely, the effect, ripened by hours of solitude, of his student life at the Tübinger-Stift and his continuing close association (now through correspondence) with two of the great Romantic figures, Hölderlin and Schelling, Hegel's thought takes a new turn; no longer does he place his emphasis pedantically on the classics and have a cool detached approach to his subject-matter. Words like "Liebe", "Leben", "Freiheit", "Vernunft", "Volk", and "Geist"with all their romantic, emotive connotations now populate his writings.

   Indicative of Hegel's change of interest and outlook is a fragment discovered by Franz Rosenzweig and entitled by him "Das älteste Systemprogramm des deutschen Idealismus".[1] The author-

---

[1]   *Sitzungsberichte der Heidelberger Akademie der Wissenschaften: Philosophisch-historisch Klasse*, VIII, 5 (1917), 1-50.

ship of this philosophical fragment is still in dispute, but one thing is clear: the manuscript in question is undoubtedly in Hegel's handwriting, and, more specifically, compares very closely with his script style in 1796 and early 1797. This piece serves as an excellent example of the intellectual influences on Hegel at this critical period, even though he probably did not write it himself. Rosenzweig thinks that Hegel copied this manifesto from Schelling. Hoffmeister agrees with him[2] and reproduces Rosenzweig's text, re-entitling it, however, "Erstes Systemprogramm des Deutschen Idealismus".[3] The most recent research on this fragment, however, affirms its Hegelian authorship.[4]

This short fragment outlines the requirements of the new philosophy. It will not find its inspiration in the science or statecraft of the day; they are too constricting and treat men as machines ("Wir müssen über den Staat hinaus!"). What is needed is freedom and utter independence:

Absolute Freiheit aller Geister, die die intellektuelle Welt in sich tragen und weder Gott noch Unsterblichkeit *ausser sich* suchen dürfen.[5]

The author then says that the leading idea uniting *(verschwistert)* Truth and Goodness is Beauty.

It is the remainder of this declaration, however, that is of special interest. It is claimed that the philosopher must possess an aesthetic

---

[2] Hoffmeister, *Dokumente*, 455.

[3] Hoffmeister, *Dokumente*, 219-221. Schelling may have in turn copied it from Hölderlin, since the former was strongly influenced by him at the time. The best-known proponent of this view is Ernst Cassirer who discusses the problem in his essay on Hölderlin in *Idee und Gestalt* (Berlin: B. Cassirer, 1921), 128-132. Nicolai Hartmann echoes this view, and brings up the matter in a footnote in the section on Hölderlin in his *Die Philosophie des Deutschen Idealismus* (2nd ed. unrev.; Berlin: Walter de Gruyter & Co., 1960) Part I, 186-187. Hartmann sums the problem up as follows: "Die Frage der Urheberschaft führt zunächst auf Schelling, von diesem aber, wie es scheint, weiter auf Hölderlin zurück, dessen Besuch bei Schelling der Abfassungszeit unmittelbar vorausgeht". *Ibid.*, 186. For the latest discussion of this fragment and its importance for German idealism, see Otto Pöggeler, "Hegel, der Verfasser des Ältesten Systemprogramms des Deutschen Idealismus", *Hegel-Studien*, Supplement 4 (1969), 18-32.

[4] Pöggeler, *Hegel-Studien*, 18-19.

[5] Hoffmeister, *Dokumente*, 220.

power and sensibility just like a poet. Without it men are *Buch-stabenphilosophen* ("philosophers of the mere letter"). The coming *Philosophie des Geistes* (also referred to as the *Geschichte der Mensch-heit*) is to be an aesthetic philosophy. Without an aesthetic sense, one cannot approach matters with the proper spirit and ingenuity. Without being "geistreich", true understanding of ideas is obscured, since such spiritless people live only in the world of the letter, of tables and indices. [6]

It is claimed that poetry will do the best: she will be the instructress of humanity and will outlive all the other sciences and arts. Poetry alone can mediate the needs of both the masses and the philosophers; what is required is a "monotheism of reason and heart, a polytheism of imagination and art". [7] The only form of poetry that will supply the necessary concrete, sentient power, for this "sinnliche Religion" is a new kind of mythology, in the service of ideas: *a mythology of Reason;*

wir müssen eine neue Mythologie haben, diese Mythologie aber muss im Dienste der Ideen stehen, sie muss eine Mythologie der *Vernunft* werden. [8]

This mythology must be philosophical and the people made rational *(vernünftig);* philosophy must become mythological, in order to make philosophers aware of concrete, sensual life. Only then will eternal unity reign between the philosophers and the masses. There will be no more oppression and the universal freedom and equality of spirits will be a reality ("Dann herrscht allgemeine Freiheit und Gleichheit der Geister!") [9]

A more earnest manifesto for the Romantic movement can hardly be imagined. Several motifs appear here most prominently

---

[6] "Man kann in nichts geistreich sein, selbst über Geschichte kann man nicht geistreich raisonieren – ohne ästhetischen Sinn. Hier soll offenbar werden, woran es eigentlich den Menschen fehlt, die keine Ideen verstehen, – und treuherzig genug gestehen, dass ihnen alles dunkel ist, sobald es über Tabellen und Register hinausgeht". Hoffmeister, *Dokumente*, 220.

[7] Hoffmeister, *Dokumente*, 220.

[8] Hoffmeister, *Dokumente*, 220.

[9] Hoffmeister, *Dokumente*, 220.

and will be developed and re-worked by Hegel himself in his later thought. First, the appeal to philosophy to go beyond the letter, beyond "kalte Buchgelehrsamkeit" is crucial. Secondly, the need for a concretely apprehended exoteric philosophy which will capture the true spirit of reality and adequately express man's universal aspirations. This new religion must be grounded in the living experience and imagination of its people and be described in dynamic terms that go beyond the pale, static relations of under-standing rather than in phrases and images which were under-standable and appropriate a few thousand years ago in Syria.[10] The phrase "a Mythology of Reason" best conveys all this for Hegel.

Hegel's demands for a new interpretation of philosophy and religion clearly reflect themselves in his new views on the role and need for language. As we turn to Hegel's main writings at this time, the need for language to have a concrete relation to a people, to go beyond the categories of *Verstand* in order to embody the more spiritual and dynamic categories of *Vernunft* and finally to avoid the deadening esoteric formulas usual to philosophy, becomes apparent.

During his *Hauslehrerjahre* in Bern and Frankfurt, Hegel was preoccupied with religious and theological matters. His interest in classical languages and civilizations waned and he turned to the origins of Christianity and the figure of Jesus. These are inter-preted in the light of his own philosophical predispositions at the time and show the development of Hegel's thought on religion and his philosophy in general. One of his earliest works of this time, *Das Leben Jesu*, points up implicitly Hegel's theme: Jesus was not understood by the Jews, not even by those sympathetic to his cause. Jesus and most of the Jews spoke two different languages because they lived in two different spiritual worlds. Jesus' followers thought that he would re-establish the kingdom of Judea, politically in-

---

[10] "die Ohren alle sieben Tage Phrasen und Bildern zu leihen, die vor einigen tausend Jahren in Syrien verständlich und am Platze waren". Cited in W. Dilthey's *Die Jugendgeschichte Hegels*, vol. IV of his *Gesammelte Schriften* (Leipzig: B. G. Teubner, 1921), 28.

dependent of Rome, and that they would be materially compensated for their hardships.[11]

However, the full implications of this problem of communication are explicitly examined by Hegel in *The Spirit of Christianity and its Fate*, written in Frankfurt in 1798-1799, and the crowning work of this period. The close connection between the cultural and social development of a people and its language and phraseology is clearly seen.

Hegel claims that John the Evangelist had the most to say about God and the relationship between God and Jesus. He contends that Jewish culture, being so poor in spiritual relationships, limited the expressive powers of John (as well as Jesus), and "forced him to avail himself of objective ties and matter-of-fact phraseology for expressing the highest spiritual realities".[12] The spiritual realm, the divine, can only be spoken of in inspired, appropriately spiritual terms. The language of reflection, of opposition between subject and object, is thoroughly inadequate to the task. John had to fight against this mode of speaking, but finally had no choice but to express himself in forms which appear outwardly as indicative of the very mentality he was opposing, since he himself belonged to the same people.

Thus the propositions at the beginning of the Gospel according to John ("In the beginning *was* the Logos; the Logos *was with* God, and God *was* the Logos; in Him *was* life".) appear to be ordinary reflective judgments, on the order of S is (or was) P. But, says Hegel, this is deceptive because such predicates are some-thing living and dynamic, though formally such propositions are not adapted to the needs of spiritual expression.[13] Language which communicates the divine can only be understood if one's spiritual background is receptive to deeper meanings. One cannot

---

[11] "sie hatten 'sich' noch nicht den geistigen Sinn des Reiches Gottes, als einer Herrschaft der Tugendgesetze unter den Menschen – zu eigen gemacht". H. Nohl, *Hegels theologische Jugendschriften* (Tübingen: J. C. B. Mohr [Paul Siebeck], 1907), 114. The Kantian influence and terminology in this work (indeed, in this citation) are apparent.
[12] Knox, *On Christianity*, 255.
[13] Knox, *On Christianity*, 256.

understand such statements with the passive powers of understanding, "because everything expressed about the divine in the
language of reflection is *eo ipso* contradictory".[14] Hegel then
launches into a complicated exegesis of the relation between the
Logos and God as implicit in the above propositions, but finally
concedes that

> However sublime the idea of God may be made here, there yet always
> remains the Jewish principle of opposing thought to reality, reason to
> sense; this principle involves the rending of life and a lifeless connection
> between God and the world, though the tie between these must be taken
> to be a living connection; and where such a connection is in question,
> *ties between the related terms can be expressed only in mystical phraseology*
> (Italics mine).[15]

One cannot hope to grasp the living, spiritual world of the Divine
with the inert categories of reflective understanding. The language
of reflection is incapable of expressing the life of the Divine.[16]

Hegel does not say that higher spiritual truths are ineffable and
inexplicable, but that our usual language and phraseology is not
appropriate to them. "What is a contradiction in the realm of the
dead is not one in the realm of the life".[17] Mystical phraseology
may be necessary, but this too is a language expressive of certain
facts and relations. Hegel never despaired of attempting to explain
any of the paradoxes of faith and never lapsed into obscurantism
or *Schwärmerei*. A few pages after the above discussion, he even
attempts an explanation of the Trinity. Language *per se* is not a
stranger to the realm of spirit; there is a comprehension beyond
that of the categories of "Verstand" and the language which

---

14   Knox, *On Christianity*, 256.
15   Knox, *On Christianity*, 259. The criticism of Kantianism, as well as Judaism, is apparent in this citation. Jesus no longer appears as a proponent of
Kantian ethics and epistemology, but as a strong critic.
16   Dilthey sums this up well when he says, "Wie die Lebensbeziehungen der
Liebe in der fremden Form des Begriffs stets den falschen Charakter eines Ge-
bots annehmen, so wird jeder Ausdruck über Göttliches in der Form der
Reflexion widersinnig. Man muss das Göttliche mit eigenem tiefen Geist
auffassen...." *Die Jugendgeschichte Hegels*, 102.
17   Knox, *On Christianity*, 261.

embodies them. It is seen for Hegel in the relation of a people
(Volk) to its God, and a people's language is the key to understanding this relationship. Language is closely related to the culture
of a people and expressive of it; language reflects the deeper spirit
of a people as well as its ordinary thought patterns. Not only
general rules of a language should be considered, but also the
unique cultural elements in it as well. During his years in Jena,
Hegel closely examined the nature and implications of this relation
of a language to its people.

B. JENA: THE SEARCH FOR A LANGUAGE FOR PHILOSOPHY

In 1805, in a letter to Johann Heinrich Voss, author of the celebrated
German translation of Homer, Hegel says that he would like to
"try to teach philosophy to speak German". Once this is accomplished, he continues, "it will be infinitely more difficult to give
shallowness the appearance of profound speech".[18] In these few
words, Hegel pinpoints the relation between language and philosophy. The task is two fold: philosophy must speak idiomatically
and exoterically, and this in turn will obviate the impressive, but
really meaningless terminology of present-day thought.

In seeking flexible, dynamic means for expressing his philosophy,
Hegel is very eager that this new "language of philosophy" should
appropriate the materials and modes familiar to his general cultural
audience. Hegel prefaces the above remarks to Voss with one of
his recurrent observations concerning the need for a deep connection between a language and its people:

Luther has made the Bible speak German; you, Homer – the greatest
present that can be given to a people; for a people is barbarous and

---

[18]   Cited from W. Kaufmann, *Hegel: Reinterpretation, Texts, and Commentary*
(Garden City, N. Y.: Doubleday & Company, Inc., 1965), 314. In this letter,
Hegel expresses his disdain for "... the mischief of formalism which is practiced
at present by ignorance, especially with the help of a terminology behind which
it is hiding..." *Ibid.*

does not consider the excellent things it knows as its own property until it gets to know them in its own language;[19]

He states this even more strongly in one of his "Jena-Aphorisms",

To speak in *its own* language is one of the supreme moments of cultural development; a people belongs to itself. Away with alien things, even Latin letters![20]

Not only should a people have its own language, but even its own lettering!

Hegel is not pleading for the banishment of Latin script or of foreign languages in general. Such sentiments should not be interpreted as a stridently nationalistic plea for German cultural purity. This aphorism is only a trenchant expression of Hegel's desire for a familiar cultural universe out of which philosophy may grow. As he later says, there is a need for breaking down the "partition between the language of philosophy and that of ordinary consciousness: we have to overcome the reluctance against thinking what we are familiar with".[21] One cannot philosophize in a strange tongue with abstract symbols.[22]

---

[19] Kaufmann, *Hegel*, 314.

[20] Hoffmeister, *Dokumente*, 369.

[21] Hoffmeister, *Dokumente*, 371. The translation of this passage is taken from W. Wallace, *Prolegomena to the Study of Hegel's Philosophy and especially of his Logic*, (2nd ed. rev.; Oxford: Oxford University Press, 1894), 8.

[22] The need for Germans to develop an adequate vocabulary in order to philosophize in their own language was a theme of Leibniz's German writings. He bemoaned the lack of logical and metaphysical terms in particular, but warned against the wholesale importation of needed words from foreign languages. Such corruption of a language usually has lead to its destruction and the enslavement of its speakers (e.g., the Anglo-Saxons in England). Leibniz therefore exhorts the Germans to search out the necessary words from their own rich cultural and linguistic heritage. These thoughts are elaborated by Leibniz in "Von deutscher Sprachpflege. Unvorgreifliche Gedanken betreffend die Ausübung und Verbesserung der deutschen Sprache", *Muttersprache und völkische Gesinnung*, Vol. I of G. W. Leibniz, *Deutsche Schriften*, ed. W. Schmied-Kowarzik (Leipzig: F. Meiner, 1916), 25-54. In a companion piece, "Ermahnung an die Deutschen, ihren Verstand und ihre Sprache besser zu üben", Leibniz dwells on another theme that became a favorite of Hegel's – the importance of Luther's translation of the Bible for the development of the

Many of Hegel's thoughts on the need for a proper philosophical language are recorded by Karl Rosenkranz in his lengthy citations of Hegel's Jena lectures.[23] Hegel's polemic against the misuse of the terminology of Schelling's *Naturphilosophie* is worthy of special note. He calls it an affected kind of mysticism which tries to use common sense-images *(Vorstellungen)* to master the depths of reality and ends up only convulsing within itself, never arriving at any clear decisive conclusions.[24] Hegel then states that the proper element for this purpose is the universal whose concepts *(Begriffe)* can be fixed or established partly by means of *philosophical terminology.*

Hegel then launches into an attack on the manner in which philosophical terminology was arrived at in his day; it is this discussion which is especially relevant to our interests. The misuse of philosophical terms can lead to a greater danger, Hegel believes, than that *"Begrifflosigkeit"* which he attacks in Schelling's followers. The main reason for this is that so many words have been imported from Greek and Latin, instead of using familiar German ones. "It is truly proper to the highest cultural level of a people *to be able to say everything in its own language".*[25] The danger in using foreign words is that the concepts so denoted appear strange and irrelevant to actual and current *(gegenwärtigen)* concerns. Yet ordinary abstract German words such as *"Sein"* and *"Grosse"* are felt to be unworthy of expressing and grasping the world beyond our usual one. This "hohe Jenseits" or "übersinnliche Welt" seems alien to our everyday life and its common conceptualizing.[26] Yet, Hegel says, such an outlook is conducive to viewing philosophy and its language as something irrelevant to our lives. The objects

---

German language and, in this connection, the correlation between the intellectual progress and freedom of a people and the progress and power of its language. *Ibid.*, 1-24.

[23]   *G. W. F. Hegels Leben*, 178-198. This section is entitled by Rosenkranz: "Didaktische Modification des Systems".

[24]   Rosenkranz, *Hegels Leben*, 181-183.

[25]   Rosenkranz, *Hegels Leben*, 183.

[26]   Rosenkranz, *Hegels Leben*, 183.

of abstract thought must have concrete meaning for us *(für uns)* and not just reside objectively *(an sich)* in some impressively overarching, but esoteric network of ideas. Human thought and spirit are present everywhere and express themselves even in the ordinary concrete language of the people,[27] but the philosophers ignore these possible forms of expression and have recourse to strange terminology. Our thought is not yet at home in its own language because of a blind awe for "imported" and alien words.[28] The evil of this "imported" terminology is two-fold; that a people does not have, as yet, its own terminology to express certain ideas is unfortunate. What upsets Hegel, however, is that the perverse and indiscriminate use of alien terms leads to an *empty formalism* which deprives conceptual thought of all life and movement. Furthermore, it makes it easy to pass off nonsense and trivia as deep and difficult philosophizing, since one is speaking in a language people really do not understand.[29] In a word, people begin to think they are really studying philosophy, really being "profound", when they use big words. Hegel manifests his disdain for this procedure with a biting criticism of Kantian terminology. It seemed at first, Hegel says, very difficult to use correctly such phrases as *a priori*, synthetic judgments, synthetic unity of apperception, etc. But such a deluge *(Schwall)* of terms disappears as quickly as it came, because as soon as such language is mastered, the secret is revealed; namely, that very common thoughts are hidden behind such terminological bugbears.[30]

Hegel's main theme concerns the philosophical mischief created by the wedding of contemporary *Naturphilosophie* to Schellingian terminology. Hegel is at pains to dissociate Schelling's own ideas from the formalism of his followers. (Schelling himself cannot be accused, since he had a good philosophic sense, and in fact showed

[27]   Rosenkranz, *Hegels Leben*, 183: "der Geist selbst *allenthalben* lebt und dass er in unserer unmittelbaren Volkssprache seine Formen ausdrückt".
[28]   Rosenkranz, *Hegels Leben*, 183-184.
[29]   Rosenkranz, *Hegels Leben*, 184.
[30]   Hegel says of such language that "*sich sehr gemeine Gedanken hinter solchem Popanz von Ausdruck verstecken*". Rosenkranz, *Hegels Leben*, 184.

himself free from this very terminology, now misunderstood, since he used a new one each time he expounded his thought!). He attacks the superficiality of their thoughts, hidden behind a weighty *("zentnerschweren")* prose.[31]

Rosenkranz concludes by noting that Hegel's strongest censure was reserved for those who felt a special genius was demanded to study philosophy, thus making it the preserve of an elect few. His objection to the romantic-intuitionist view of philosophy is that it values private imagination above public reason. In Hegel's words, "philosophy, as the *Science of Reason* – by the universal manner of its being – is, by its very nature, for *everyone*".[32]

Words and ideas which have not arisen out of the common language of a people and its experiences usually lead to a stilted, spiritless approach devoid of true intellectual content. Philosophy expressed in such a fashion has no universal communicative power and its recondite forms usually relegate it to the province of a few. However, truth is not one thing for the Germans – since they have one language and culture – and another for the French, and so forth. There is only one true philosophy because there is only one true reason, but the avenue for genuinely appropriating these truths must be one's own language, since through it the cultural character and intellectual level of a people is best reflected. Many of Hegel's later illustrations, especially in the *Enzyklopädie* and the *Vorlesungen über die Philosophie der Geschichte* point out the close connection between the intellectual and cultural backwardness of a people and the language it spoke. Hegel, like many of his contemporaries, believed that there was a reciprocal relationship between the language a people spoke and the level of its intellectual and philosophical progress.[33]

---

[31]   Rosenkranz, *Hegels Leben*, 184-185.
[32]   Rosenkranz, *Hegels Leben*, 186.
[33]   An excellent example of this view, especially popular at the end of the 18th century, is recorded among Hegel's juvenilia. This is an excerpt that he copied from Moses Mendelssohn's essay, "Über die Frage: Was heisst aufklären?" As Hegel wrote it: "Die Sprache eines Volkes ist die beste Anzeige seiner Bildung, der Kultur sowohl als der Aufklärung, der Ausdehnung sowohl als der Stärke nach". Hoffmeister, *Dokumente*, 141.

C. TRUE LANGUAGE: THE PRODUCT OF A PEOPLE

Towards the end of the first draft of his "Philosophie des Geistes"[34] Hegel devotes several pages to discussing the various elements which collectively constitute the spirit of a people *(Volksgeist)* and its institutions. The first of these is language. Hegel claims that true language, as well as understanding and reason, exist only as the products or acts of a people. Only as such a product can language be the ideally existent form of mind or Spirit. Through language, a people expresses or articulates its own essence and being. Language is the common medium in which human institutions and rationality itself find their initial external existence, because through it individual consciousness recognizes itself in another. True speech is attained only through the presence of a common universe of discourse and meaning, possible only in a people *(Volk)*.[35] Hegel seems to be arguing here in a circle: on the one hand, a people cannot have its own identity and independence unless it has its own language, yet, on the other, a language, a community of discourse, exists only within a pre-existent community of individuals. Hegel meets this problem of circularity by arguing that the language of the individual in effect is reconstructed, transcended when it becomes the language of a people – a truly national language. In fact, language only fulfills its role (its *Begriff*, in Hegel's terms), as the basis for the communication and universalization of the experiences of various individuals within a people *(Volk)*.[36]

---

[34] *Jenenser Realphilosophie, I,* 235-241.

[35] "Die vorhergehenden Potenzen [Sprache, Arbeit, Anerkennung] sind überhaupt ideale; sie sind erst existierend in einem Volke; *die Sprache ist nur als Sprache eines Volkes, ebenso Verstand und Vernunft.* Nur als Werk eines Volks ist *die Sprache die ideelle Existenz des Geistes,* in welcher er sich ausspricht, was er seinem Wesen [nach] und in seinem Sein ist. Sie ist ein Allgemeines, an sich Anerkanntes, im Bewusstsein aller auf dieselbe Weise Widerhallendes; jedes sprechende Bewusstsein wird unmittelbar darin zu einem andern Bewusstsein. Sie wird ebenso ihrem Inhalte nach erst in einem Volke zur wahren Sprache, zum Aussprechen [dessen], was Jeder meint". *Jenenser Realphilosophie, I,* 235.

[36] "Die Sprache wird also auf diese Weise in einem Volke rekonstruiert, dass sie als das ideele Ver [nichten] des Äussern [viz., nature] selbst ein *Äusseres* ist,

Initially, however, consciousness is unaware that its language reflects an identity with, and self-recognition through, other consciousnesses. The subjectivity of the arbitrary naming of brute objects of experience must be transcended and the possibility of genuine communication among individual consciousnesses recognized. Language represents a potential or ideal form of community mediating and thus transcending the arbitrariness and subjectivity of individual experience and expression. Although language *ab initio* has its own existence (its *fürsichsein*) within a community of consciousnesses, the individual consciousnesses within the community do not yet realize that their mode of expression, of speaking, is in itself *(an sich)* an objectification of the very essence of their common rationality, or in other words, the first concrete manifestation of *Geist*. Language is seen simply as the means for immediately externalizing or pronouncing what is internally felt or imagined.[37] It is seen as an immediate extension of the physical world, externalizing in a natural fashion what is internal. But as linguistic communication develops among different consciousnesses, the possibility of appreciating the true nature of language, and concomitantly understanding and reason, also develops. Then consciousness breaks out of its immediate natural setting and becomes in reality what it hitherto was only formally or ideally: a member of a group which identifies itself with other members who share his common universe of discourse. Language is then no longer merely an ideal *external*ization of an individual's picture of his world, but is the *internal* mediating element among individuals within a genuine community. Language now fulfills its *Begriff* as tangibly, existentially representing a common universe of experience and discourse. The language of a people embodies its common experiences and ideals

---

das vernichtet, aufgehoben werden muss, um zur bedeutenden Sprache zu werden, zu dem, was sie an sich, ihrem Begriffe nach ist;..." *Jenenser Realphilosophie I*, 236.

[37] "Die Sprache ist ihrem Wesen nach für sich selbst vorhanden, ideell gesetzte Natur, und sie ist gleichsam blosse Form; sie ist nicht ein Produzieren, sondern die blosse Form des Äusserlichmachens was schon produziert ist, wie es gesprochen werden muss". *Jenenser Realphilosophie I*, 235.

in a manner which makes true *Bildung* possible. When one member of a society can communicate with another in such a language, he is recognized by that other individual as representing and articulating their common world of experience. Only then is genuine inter-subjectivity possible: the condition Hegel sets in the *Phänomenologie* for entrance into the realm of Spirit.

Hegel's discussion in this first draft of his "Philosophie des Geistes" is admittedly quite sketchy and at times not completely coherent. But this short section presents *in nuce* several assumptions necessary for understanding Hegel's treatment of the interrelation-ships of consciousness, language and society. Hegel's pithy state-ments in this draft give us valuable clues to understanding the role of these three factors in the overall development of the *Phäno-menologie des Geistes*, to which we now return.

D. THE INDIVIDUAL AND THE PROBLEM OF LANGUAGE

The transition from self-consciousness as Reason, as certain of being itself the ultimate source and standard of reality (a position which Hegel calls Idealism), to Spirit includes several sections in the *Phänomenologie des Geistes* that are usually neglected. These portions include a scathing attack on two pseudo-sciences that enjoyed great popularity in Hegel's day: physiognomy and phre-nology. Hegel criticizes these "sciences" in the context of portraying selfconsciousness' development out of its own immediate natural environment. In the process, Hegel makes several interesting com-ments about the nature of language for individual consciousness.[38]

---

[38] *Phänomenologie*, 227-254; Baillie, 338-372. Hegel entitles this section: "Observation of the Relation of Self-Consciousness to its Immediate Actuality – Physiognomy and Phrenology" (*Beobachtung der Beziehung des Selbstbewusst-seins auf seine unmittelbare Wirklichkeit; Physiognomik und Schädellehre*). The problem at hand is how the mind of self-consciousness immediately expresses or externalizes itself. It is one variation on that recurring problematic theme in philosophy: the nature of the relation of the mind to the body.

Unfortunately, we cannot be more systematic concerning this stage of the *Phänomenologie* and Hegel's philosophy of nature in general. Our inability to

Language (or labor) is an immediate activity because it is supposed to reveal directly man's inner thought and character. It is
primarily through the organ of speech that a man actualizes and
manifests his inner being and intentions.[39] Yet as soon as man
reveals himself through speech or action, a dialectical situation
arises. Man expresses himself so that others will understand and
recognize him. Yet his words or actions, as soon as they are uttered
or performed, gain an external existence all their own, an existence
which can be misunderstood or manipulated by others.

When this happens the individual's inner character is distorted;
he may appear in a different light to different people. Also the
speaking or acting individual may feel that he has to express himself
in one way in order to be understood in another. In either case, a
man's words and deeds, it turns out, do not immediately and
necessarily reflect his true inner being because once he has expressed
himself, he has no final control over the way in which such expressions, now detached, will be taken.

On the other hand, language or labor in a sense express too
much of a man's inner character or being, because people may
think that one's gestures, words or actions *are* what are being
expressed, rather than something internal. In such a case – and
here materialist and behaviourist theories come to mind – there is
no longer any inner that is being *ex*-pressed. There is just the
expression itself which is taken as all that exists.

Language and labor are outer expressions in which the individual no
longer retains possession of himself *per se*, but lets the inner get right
outside of him and surrenders it to another. Therefore one can just as
truly say that these outer expressions express the inner too much as that

---

fit "Observing Reason" more perfectly into the explanatory scheme afforded
by our thesis concerning Hegel's conception of language and its role in understanding the dialectical nature of experience, perhaps reflects the generally
unsatisfactory character of his philosophy of Nature. The latter has been
universally regarded as the weakest link in his dialectical chain.
[39] "nächst dem Organ der Sprache am meisten es ist [the hand], wodurch der
Mensch sich zur Erscheinung und Verwirklichung bringt". *Phänomenologie*,
231; Baillie, 342.

they do so too little: *too much* – because the inner itself breaks out in them, and there remains no opposition between them and it; they not only give an *expression* of the inner, but immediately are the inner itself; *too little* – because in speech and action the inner turns itself into an other, and thereby puts itself at the mercy of the element of change, which transforms the spoken word and the accomplished act, and makes something else out of them than they are in and for themselves as actions of a particular determinate individual.[40]

Further on, Hegel amplifies these remarks by comparing the process of expression to that of signification which he discussed at length in his early drafts of his "Philosophie des Geistes". The problem with anything expressed or externalized in terms of speech or action is that, although it has its source and justification from one particular individual, words and actions carry in themselves no tag of definite ownership or meaning. They are only symbols or arbitrary signs that have to be given meaning through agreed conventions. But surely there are better ways to determine the inner character and being of someone than reliance on conventional symbols which have varying meanings.[41]

Self-consciousness as Reason, for Hegel, is aware that it is basically at one with its world and that is cognitive categories truly reflect reality. Yet, as we have seen above, individual self-consciousness is unable to express its universal being and knowledge in terms which are concrete, enduring, univocal and universally understood. The latter occurs only when each self-consciousness

---

[40] *Phänomenologie*, 229; Baillie, 340. In the *Enzyklopädie*, Hegel says, "Language itself is exposed to the fate of serving just as much to conceal as to reveal human thoughts". Zusatz to §411, *System der Philosophie. Dritter Teil*, 252; *Hegel's Philosophy of Mind*, 151.

[41] "Dieses Äussre, obzwar eine Sprache des Individuums, die es an ihm selbst hat, ist zugleich als Zeichen etwas Gleichgültiges gegen den Inhalt, den es bezeichnen sollte, so wie das, welches sich das Zeichen setzt, gleichgültig gegen dieses". *Phänomenologie*, 251, Baillie, 368.

Hegel does not think that words have any intrinsic univocal meaning, but for purposes of continuing the dialectical schema of the *Phänomenologie*, he does show the problems that such a view creates for communication (Cf. the problem of other minds in English philosophy). The importance of developing certain contextual universal rules – still however grounded ultimately in arbitrary convention – was pointed out in Hegel's discussion on demonstratives in Chapter III.

realizes that it gains universal reality and meaning for itself only through the recognition and interaction with other such individuals. Only through relating to others can I ultimately relate to myself and to my world. But this in turn is possible only if there is a concrete universal underlying reality or substance in which all individual self-consciousnesses are grounded. Hegel finds the latter in the ethos of a nation.[42]

The universal basis for communication and self-recognition among various independently existing individuals are the customs and laws of a nation. The ethos and social order here referred to evolved naturally so that each individual only gradually becomes aware of the fact that he microcosmically reflects the universal customs and sentiments of his people, and gains his own identity only through participation in this medium. Hegel now devotes a substantial portion of his work to analyzing the process whereby individual self-consciousness realizes that the source of identity and true knowledge is to be found in a society of individuals concretely and consciously working out their own collective destiny. Thus the individual comes to realize the implications of his hitherto merely immediate and natural existence in a particular social ethos; now he explicitly becomes aware of the realm of Spirit in which he dwells.

Spirit is the *ethos* of a *people* in so far as it is the *immediate truth;* [it is] a world [present] in one individual. Spirit must progress beyond the consciousness of what it is now immediately; it must transcend the simple beauty of its ethos, and pass through a series of lifepatterns to attain knowledge of itself.[43]

As we turn to the level of Spirit in the *Phänomenologie*, we will no longer be dealing with individual consciousness and its forms of intellectual expression, but rather with collective ways of life or world-views.

---

[42]   "diese allgemeine Substanz redet ihre *allgemeine Sprache* in den Sitten und Gesetzen seines Volks". *Phänomenologie*, 258; Baillie, 377.
[43]   *Phänomenologie*, 315; Baillie, 460.

These [life-patterns] are distinguished from the preceding ones in that they are authentic spiritual forms, actual world-patterns, rather than mere forms of consciousness.[44]

The ultimate authenticity and universality of consciousness' earlier experiences and the ability to detect the dialectical nature of such experiences in the language used to express them, is grounded in understanding the more developed, spiritual forms of expression, as found in culture, art, religion and finally, philosophy. The objects of consciousness' world are now seen as products of its own self-conscious process of experience. The dialectical qualities of such a process – present at all levels in the realm of Spirit – are resident in the various ways in which self-consciousness talks about its experiences. Hegel consistently refers to the type of linguistic expression used to describe self-consciousness in order to illustrate the dialectical nature of its experience. Finally, it is important to note, in the next few chapters, how the transition from one level of Spirit to another is expressed by a reference to and analysis of certain characteristic statements made by self-consciousness, viz., as a cultured, artistic, religious or philosophical being.

[44]   *Phänomenologie*, 315; Baillie, 460.

V

LANGUAGE AS THE MEDIUM OF CULTURE
AND MORALITY

In turning to actual world-patterns *("Gestalten einer Welt")* rather
than forms of individual consciousness *("Gestalten des Bewusstseins")*, one encounters a new set of categories for Hegel. Consciousness is no longer alienated from its immediate physical
setting. It has come to realize that its mental categories adequately
reflect the truth of the outside world. Self-consciousness, however,
is aware that it is unable to express or assert itself in a fashion that
is universally understood and respected. It requires a means for
communicating with others and thus gaining an understanding of
its own individual existence. The problem is no longer strictly a
theoretical one, but a practical and social one.

The community of understanding and universal recognition
which individual self-consciousness seeks is ideally represented in
its speech, which others comprehend. Such language is based upon
a common universe of experience which is henceforth made explicit.
Through speaking, consciousness transcends its own isolated
existence and realizes that its experiences are not arbitrary or
unique, but part of a larger community or ethos. Language is the
first and most immediate existential form of intersubjectivity. In
the final sections of the last chapter, we traced Hegel's treatment
of the transition of individual consciousness to national consciousness through the medium of language.

Though self-consciousness now sees itself as a member of a
larger community, at least superficially understood and recognized
by other self-consciousnesses, it still seeks to determine its exact
relationship to them and its purpose in this society. Consciousness
feels itself estranged, not immediately at home, in its newly found
social world, and attempts to overcome, or at least come to terms

with that feeling of alienation.

A. HEGEL'S THEORY OF CULTURE

At the earliest stages of learning, consciousness is made aware of its own existence by the creation of a distance between it and what was hitherto its immediate, natural surroundings. The creation of such a distance or alienation is the condition of any education.[1] In explaining the above process, Hegel uses two words which occur together often in his later thought. These are *Bildung*, which can be translated as education, culture, civilization, or more simply as development, constitution or formation, and *Entfremdung* – estrangement or alienation. Only through a sense of alienation can consciousness gain the necessary distance whereby it becomes aware of a situation or fact that otherwise it never thought about. Such a process occurs on various levels and with varying complexity for Hegel, and it is for this reason that the word *Bildung* has so many meanings. Initially, *Bildung* refers to theoretical education or the gaining of an awareness of certain categories (at first, those of Understanding; later, those of Reason) as a means of interpreting the external world. Later *Bildung* takes on the further meaning of culture or civilization; for Hegel, the latter has certain characteristics that make the situation of consciousness in *Bildung* especially poignant. It is this level of *Bildung* which Hegel examines at length in a large section of the *Phänomenologie des Geistes* called "Self-Alienated Spirit: Culture" *("Der sich entfremdete Geist; Bildung")*.[2]

This level of culture or human development has certain identifiable features. These characteristics of *Bildung* form a pattern which recurs, according to Hegel, periodically in human history, though in different forms. He discusses the nature of *Bildung* at length in several works after the *Phänomenologie*, such as the be-

---

[1]   This process was described at length in Chapter I.
[2]   *Phänomenologie*, 347-376; Baillie, 507-548.

ginning of Civil Society and class distinction in his *Grundlinien der Philosophie des Rechts* and in his treatment of the Sophists in his *Geschichte der Philosophie*. From these as well as other places, we gain a coherent picture of what Hegel means when he talks of *Bildung*.[3]

The state or process of *Bildung* in all its advanced forms is characterized first of all by an individualistic attitude which arises out of the awareness of oneself as a person with certain rights and opinions. Consciousness is no longer submerged in the immediacy of its own ethos, but is aware of its own independent existence.[4] At the same time, however, that immediate certainty and truth that was grounded in the universal medium of an ethos is lost. Consciousness, while utilizing the categories of thought which it had gained at an earlier stage of *Bildung*, sees its thoughts and opinions as not necessarily reflecting any universally accepted truths. On the one hand, consciousness is an individual whose thoughts embody certain universal forms, while, on the other, it is estranged – practically and theoretically – from its world. In this realm of culture there are no accepted truths or unquestioned values.

Such a condition, according to Hegel, is ultimately beneficial for human intellectual development because it makes consciousness aware of the need for defending its own beliefs, beliefs which it hitherto accepted unquestioningly as part of a universal ethos. Consciousness in culture learns to see things from other angles

---

[3] It should be noted that *Bildung* has a further and final meaning for Hegel. It is this meaning which is usually associated with the (German) Romantic tradition and its *Bildungsroman*. Examples of the latter include Goethe's *Wilhelm Meisters Lehrjahre* (1795/1796). In such literature, the hero is educated through a series of developing experiences. So here in the *Phänomenologie*, consciousness undergoes a series of experiences which constitute its own *Bildung*. In the Preface, Hegel speaks of *"der sich bildende Geist"*. See W. Kaufmann, *Hegel*, 381. Josiah Royce relies heavily upon this interpretation of the *Phänomenologie des Geistes* as a *Bildungsroman*. See his *Lectures on Modern Idealism* (New Haven: Yale University Press, 1964), 147-156.

[4] "Die *Bildung*... ist der absolute Durchgangspunkt zu der, nicht mehr unmittelbaren, natürlichen, sondern geistigen, ebenso zur Gestalt der Allgemeinheit erhobenen unendlich subjektiven Substantialität der Sittlichkeit". *Grundlinien der Philosophie des Rechts*, ed. J. Hoffmeister (4th ed.; Hamburg: F. Meiner, 1955), 168-169.

and thus is better able to defend its own position. Hegel says, "A man of culture thus knows how to say something of everything, to find points of view in all".[5] Such a display of knowledge or rhetoric may only be an exercise in cleverness, but this ability to consider a matter from various perspectives enables consciousness to gain that detachment from its immediate environment that is a necessary step towards a genuine state of knowledge.

The first society to experience the effects of this world of culture, according to Hegel, were the Greeks. A relativistic and individualistic attitude towards the world was encouraged by the Sophists. People learned from them "the power of keeping the manifold points of view present to the mind, so that the wealth of categories by which an object may be considered, immediately occurs to it".[6]

The general outlook which such a period exemplifies is of special interest to us because of the role of language in culture. For Hegel, the Sophists were the first to realize the importance of categorizing things so that we may communicate our specific intent when we speak of them. Thus Hegel mentions the Sophists' interest in rhetoric:

'the Sophist is one who knows how to make men clever (δεινόν) in speech', to turn objects around and consider them from many sides. In fact, what is most striking in a cultured man or people is the art of speaking well.[7]

But mere speech does not guarantee good speaking. Cultivation or culture is necessary. One can master the rules of a language completely, but if there is no culture, there is no proper speaking.[8]

[5] Hegel, *Lectures on the History of Philosophy*, tr. E. S. Haldane (New York: Humanities Press, 1963), I, 356; *Vorlesungen über die Geschichte der Philosophie II*, Vol. XVIII of *Sämtliche Werke*, ed. H. Glockner (Stuttgart: Fr. Frommanns, 1928), 10.
[6] Haldane, *Lectures on the History of Philosophy*, I, 359; *Geschichte der Philosophie II*, 12.
[7] Haldane, *Lectures*, 12.
[8] "Aber das Blosse Sprechen macht es nicht aus, sondern die Bildung gehört dazu. Man kann eine Sprache ganz regelrecht inne haben; wenn man aber die Bildung nicht hat, so ist es nicht gut sprechen". Haldane, *Lectures*, 12.

Only when an individual has experienced the intellectual detachment, whereby he alone can gain a concrete knowledge of the proper categories, can he be called "cultured". Language, as a vehicle for communication, must always be anchored in the experience of a specific world view in order to be genuine and have universal validity. Otherwise, it can be misinterpreted or thought to reflect merely private, idiosyncratic views.

We now turn to the actual section on Culture in the *Phänomenologie* to examine in more detail the nature of consciousness' alienation and the role of language as reflecting this estrangement and as a means for overcoming it. In this section, Hegel analyzes the various types of language, judgment and attitude that interact and develop out of this new level of experience for consciousness. Until now we have given a somewhat composite picture of the relationship between *Bildung*, alienation and language. It is necessary to examine Hegel's analysis of the problem of language and communication in a society of alienated individuals in more detail so that one can appreciate the degree of interest and sophistication that he brings to it. Such an examination of Hegel's feeling for the problem of communication and his discernment of the various kinds of language and expression present in a society will further increase our understanding of the role of language in his thought.

B. ALIENATION OF SELF-CONSCIOUSNESS IN CULTURE

Individual consciousness develops an awareness of abstract categories of thought by being alienated from its immediate environment. Just as theoretical knowledge is gained by such a process, so higher forms of knowledge and consciousness for Hegel – here specifically cultural and ethical – are gained by this process of alienation, where self-consciousness is forced by the logic of its own experience to renounce its own natural immediate existence. Self-consciousness can gain a genuine awareness of the nature of interpersonal relations and the workings of society and state only through the self-alienation that occurs through Culture. It is through this formative process that consciousness gains its true individual identity and effectiveness.[9]

Immersed in the immediacy of its ethos *(Sittlichkeit)*, consciousness lived in a safe world of accepted values and universal truths. Such societies have a form of language, Hegel claims, which reflects this natural cohesiveness and underlying unity. The language of such a social order is the language of law and command (*Gesetz und Befehl*). Each person has a certain role and destiny which he fulfills, willingly or otherwise. "The language of ethos-oriented Spirit is law and simple command and complaint, which is but a tear shed over necessity".[10]

Upon entering the realm of culture, consciousness is aware of its own individuality and the need for establishing the congruence of its own practical and moral beliefs with those of the governing power. Consciousness develops a set of polar categories – "good" and "bad" – which denote identity with the state and its interests and resources, or estrangement from them respectively. These value judgments are grounded in the individual's relation to what it takes to be the ground and source of being and value: the State. By identifying with the Power of the State or its Wealth, consciousness hopes to overcome that alienation which arises when it is thrust out of the immediacy of its own ethos. The process of cultivation begins when an individual gains sufficient detachment to make value-judgments concerning its world and what is good or bad for *itself*. It assumes that its notion of what is "good" or true coincides with certain universal standards. The first type of language that Hegel mentions in this section is that of advice, which imparts certain abstract truths about what is universally best to the leaders of the State (*"das allgemeine Beste"*).[11]

Consciousness believes that the interest of the State is its own and so it dedicates itself to the State through word and action. But consciousness soon realizes that what it thought to be "good" – i.e., at one with state-power and wealth – is really "bad", since it

---

9   *Phänomenologie*, 351; Baillie, 514-515.
10   *Phänomenologie*, 458; Baillie, 651.
11   *Phänomenologie*, 361; Baillie, 528.

loses its own identity in its devotion to the state. In gaining its *raison d'etre*, it has lost its own individuality. What is characteristic of the realm of culture is the emergence of an awareness on the part of consciousness of the gap between its judgment and expression and its experience. Such an "honest" or "noble" individual who identified goodness with the interest of the State now becomes "base", since it realizes that its former attitude resulted in its sacrificing its own individual identity or existence. What was once "good" is now "bad" and vice versa; none of its opinions or judgments are anchored in objective reality – only subjective attitudes prevail;[12] nevertheless, only through such an experience can consciousness arrive at a true understanding of subjectivity, both in himself and others: for Hegel, a necessary step in the development of a genuine ethical and spiritual outlook.

C. LANGUAGE AS SELF-ASSERTION

Until now the language of individual consciousness has been a medium for apprehending various theoretical categories. Language has been viewed as the formal clothing of implicitly *(an sich)* existing categories. It expressed these categories, serving as the means whereby consciousness was made explicitly *(für sich)* aware of their existences. Now, language takes on a reality of its own for alienated consciousness. Words no longer describe an external situation or an internal state *per se*, but also represent the sheer utterance of self-assertion. Language, hitherto an expression of the dialectical development of the categories of experience, now gains an existence and force in its own right. In the mere act of speaking out, language performs its function of enabling the individual ego to relate itself to its social world, by gaining the recognition and attention of others and thus transcending its own private existence. The very act of speaking mediates between a particular ego and the world with which it seeks to identify.

[12]   *Phänomenologie*, 353; Baillie, 517.

Here, however, it [language] receives as content the form which it is itself, and is valid as *language*. It is the power of speaking as such, which does what has to be done. Language is in effect the *existence (Dasein)* of pure self as self. In it the *self-oriented individuality* of self-consciousness as such enters into existence, so that it exists *for others*.[13]

Language represents the external embodiment *(Dasein)* of ego itself. Individual consciousness finds in the act of speaking a way of adequately projecting itself into the world. "Language... contains the ego in its purity; it alone pronounces the 'I', the 'I' itself".[14]

Representing subjectivity itself, language, throughout this section and later ones, becomes the actual medium of spirit. Language is the existential form of Spirit itself because it embodies this mediating process between the individual and his world.[15] Through language, consciousness effectively estranges itself from its own private world and commits itself to the power of the State. The various tensions that arise from this relation between the individual and the state are characterized, for Hegel, by the kind of speech that consciousness uses. It is at this level of *Bildung* that Hegel explicitly defines the relationship of language to self-consciousness as Spirit: each stage of intellectual development, each determinate form of Spirit, has its distinct language, its particular expression.[16]

Consciousness, in speaking out, seeks a means whereby it could assert its own existence *(für sich sein)* and thus identify with and commit itself to the outside world. In consciousness' assertion of self through speech its particular ego, however, is expressed and externalized in terms which are of universal application. "*I* is *this* I, but equally a *universal* one".[17] The private language and world of the individual is now transcended and at one with those

---

[13] *Phänomenologie*, 362; Baillie, 530. Jean Hyppolite's French translation was consulted, *La Phénoménologie de l'esprit* (Paris: Aubier, 1941), II, 69. Hyppolite's translation will be cited whenever it has been consulted.
[14] *Phänomenologie*, 362; Baillie, 530.
[15] *Phänomenologie*, 363; Baillie, 532.
[16] "Die beiden Momente, zu welchen beide Seiten gereinigt, und die daher Momente der Sprache sind..." *Phänomenologie*, 364; Baillie, 532.
[17] *Phänomenologie*, 362; Baillie, 530.

who recognize him. Hegel likens this universalizing nature of first person singular pronouns to a kind of contagion: *everyone* can use these words. (In "Sense-Certainty" we saw how terms like "I", "This", "Here", and "Now", while referring to particular subject, objects or states, in fact have a universal or non-specific meaning and usage.) The meaning of such words "spreads" out equally among all, thereby transcending and cancelling out the individuality and particular reference of such pronouncements.[18] Henceforth, self-consciousness exists only as someone recognized and understood within society. By sacrificing its individual isolated existence, by "dying" through the act of self-assertion, consciousness gains universal recognition.

D. THE LANGUAGES OF ALIENATION

Honest or noble consciousness thought it possible to return to that certainty and stability which it previously possessed in its particular ethos. Its actions, thought and language reflected this hope, whether as service, sacrifice or advice. It assumed that certain standards existed, that there was an objectively grounded good and bad, a true and a false and that its role was to attune its own outlook and values to these realities. But the process of culture or civilization, according to Hegel, results in the realization on the part of consciousness that there are no such objective, universal verities. All judgments are subjective and the statements of a cultured individual do not describe or refer to any objective truths, but are only a means for personal recognition. *What* language says is no longer important; what counts is *how, why* and *to whom* it is said. Language comes into its own because it is no longer descriptive of an objective condition and therefore not determined by an objectively valid judgment concerning truth or falsity, goodness or evil.

---

[18] "*Ich*, das sich ausspricht, ist *vernommen;* es ist eine Ansteckung, worin es unmittelbar in die Einheit mit denen, für welche es da ist, übergegangen und allgemeines Selbstbewusstsein ist". *Phänomenologie*, 362-363; Baillie, 530.

Language becomes an *artifice* since it is now a tool for advice, persuasion and flattery. Initially, consciousness was alienated because it couldn't say what it meant and didn't mean what it said. Now consciousness does not *want* to say what it means or mean what it says. Hegel would agree with Conrad's definition of a diplomatic statement as one "in which everything is true, but the sentiment which seems to prompt it". Even the language of advice – which pronounced what was "universally best" – is only a mask for furthering self-interest. The noble or knight who has braved death and sacrificed himself for his king counsels with a sense of his own self-importance and interest. In reserving the right to his own opinion and his own individual will, he is, in fact, not at one with the power of the State at all. The languages of flattery and rupture (*Schmeichelei* and *Zerrissenheit*) reflect this atmosphere of estrangement in even more extreme forms. Lessing, in *Emilia Galotti* (a play with which Hegel was familiar) captures this artificial, dissimulating quality of the languages of the courtier and the diplomat. In this play, Claudia warns her daughter Emilia about the words and actions of the Prince.

The Prince is gallant. You are too little accustomed to the insignificant *[unbedeutende]* language of gallantry. In it, an act of courtesy turns into a sensation, a word of flattery into a true assertion, an idea into a wish, a wish into a design. In this language nothing sounds like everything, and in it everything is as much as nothing.[19]

Language for Hegel can embody absolute knowledge or Spirit, but it can have this truth-value only when consciousness has fully experienced the meaning of its own subjectivity and has entered into a fully understood relationship with other subjects. At one point here Hegel notes that while language is the actual means for the mediating process between the poles of consciousness and state-power, the latter has not yet attained actual self-hood or subjectivity. Therefore, "This language is not yet Spirit, as it knows and articulates itself completely".[20] Such language, however, plays a

[19]   G. E. Lessing, *Emilia Galotti*, tr. Edward Dvoretzky (New York: Frederick Ungar Publishing Co., 1962), 28.
[20]   *Phänomenologie*, 364; Baillie, 533. Hegel prefaces this statement with the

necessary role in the development of social and political consciousness (Spirit) by furthering the possibility of genuine subjectivity. The language of praise and flattery is the medium "through
which the various sides of this relationship form themselves into
active wholes".[21] That Spirit manifests itself as language and therefore as the means for the development of self-consciousness in
Culture is apparent in the following statement of Hegel:

As self-consciousness in the face of state-power had its language – or
[that] Spirit appears between these extremes as an effective means –
so it [self-consciousness] has its language in the face of wealth, and even
more so rebellion [has] its language.[22]

Through the language of flattery, noble consciousness thought that
it saw a means of identifying with the power and resources of the
king and therefore also with his subjects, thus gaining universal
recognition and personal self-certainty. But by externalizing its
own person through the language of homage and flattery, noble
consciousness begins to realize how trifling its words and actions
are. Its profession of altruism and loyalty to the established order
is, in fact, motivated strictly by self-interest and personal gain.
Talk becomes "empty" and hypocritical. No one believes what the
other is saying and if someone honestly tries to express himself,
he becomes the subject of witticisms. The point soon becomes to
dissimulate properly, to learn through speech to mask one's selfish
interests and not take anything or anyone seriously. There is no
ultimate truth or reality with which one can identify, and so, with
speech as its medium, noble consciousness becomes base.

Individual existence is now characterized as being completely
at odds with any notion of universality or objectivity. Such a condition, manifested through the language of rupture *(Zerrissenheit)*,
is the culmination of the process of culture. "It is this absolute

---

comment that this mutual relationship becomes effective "in dieser *vermittelnden
Bewegung*... deren einfaches Dasein, als *Mitte*, die Sprache ist". *Phänomenologie*,
364; Baillie, 533.

[21] *Phänomenologie*, 364; Baillie, 533.
[22] *Phänomenologie*, 370; Baillie, 540; Hyppolite, II, 77.

and universal perversion *(Verkehrung)* and alienation of reality and thought: *pure culture*".[23]

Hegel maintains that consciousness' mode of language in this state of discord or rupture[24] is consummate, and is, indeed, the "actual existential Spirit of this whole world of culture".[25] Language embodies, more than anything else, this ruptured state between consciousness as subject and the world about it. Previously meaningful words like "good", "bad" or "true" no longer have any objective referent; subjects and predicates are indifferently applied to one another.[26] Everything once thought to be good is bad and *vice versa*. The only reality is the individual who expresses these opposing or contradictory sentiments. His language is perfectly appropriate because it expresses the utter individuality and complete subjectivity of consciousness. The *Dasein* of Spirit itself is this "general speaking and disintegrative judging".[27] True subjectivity is gained in this state of *Bildung* because consciousness, through its talking and judgment, can reduce anything to a trifle with no real meaning. The attitude of consciousness is the determining factor; what is important is *how* one can manipulate and invert any point of view in a witty fashion. Being full of wit or "spirit" *(geistreich)* is how Spirit *(Geist)* now manifests itself.

Language first comes into its own as an expression of the individuality and arbitrariness of self-consciousness in alienation. Such an individual fits into a universal intellectual pattern but

---

[23] *Phänomenologie*, 370; Baillie, 541. In the word *"Verkehrung"*, Hegel is able to denote both the perverting and inverting nature of language; the English words "distortion" or "perversion" do not carry the meaning of reversing or inverting. *"Eine Verkehrung"*, it should not be forgotten, refers also to the truth-value of a statement and can be defined in a substantive fashion as an inverse proposition or misstatement.

[24] I think that "rupture" is the only adequate English word that conveys Hegel's meaning. Baillie's "disintegration" does not carry with it the meaning of a *violent* tearing away of something from something else. Hyppolite's use of the word *"dechirement"* is a perfect translation for *"Zerrissenheit"*.

[25] *Phänomenologie*, 370; Baillie, 541.

[26] *Phänomenologie*, 370; Baillie, 541.

[27] *Phänomenologie*, 372; Baillie, 542.

language here is not an expression of universal or general truths.[28] Language is first truly spiritual here because it is the perfect expression of consciousness' attempt to master itself in this state of complete alienation. Through witty expressions about the vanity and meaninglessness of everything, such a detached individual exposes the contradictions present in thought and reality itself. It is

a self which not only knows how to talk about everything, but knows how to state wittily the contradictions of the fixed essences of reality and the hard and fast distinctions of judgment – and this contradiction is their truth.[29]

By exposing the contradictory or dialectical nature of thought and reality itself, the individual in culture, through its rupturing outlook and expression, performs an essential role in the spiritual development of human consciousness. Out of this condition – pathetic for the consciousness which is experiencing it – arises the possibility of authentic individuality. By mastering the condition in which one is detached from everything and everyone, where the objects of thought and experience themselves have no inner connection or meaning, self-consciousness gains true self-hood.[30] By creatively expressing and weaving together the contradictory elements of experience, consciousness gains an insight into the nature of existence and thought themselves, and has forcefully asserted its own individuality. Now the expressions of self-consciousness, as language or any other mode, are truly spiritual forms, because they originate in a consciousness certain of itself as subject in a world of other subjects.

---

[28] The French *Philosophes* and Encyclopaedists themselves, as Hegel points out, systematized the "wisdom" of these "base" prerevolutionary types. *Phänomenologie*, 384; Baillie, 560.

[29] *Phänomenologie*, 375; Baillie, 546; Hyppolite, II, 83-84.

[30] *Phänomenologie*, 375-376; Baillie, 547.

E. LANGUAGE AND MORAL ACTION

The final section on Spirit in the *Phänomenologie*, entitled "Spirit Certain of Itself: Morality" (*"Der seiner selbst gewisse Geist, Die Moralität"*), culminates in an analysis of the "*self of consciousness, Spirit immediately certain of itself as absolute truth and being*".[31] As conscience, individual consciousness is convinced that its own outlook reflects the true nature of its actual condition. It views any action that it undertakes as part of *its* duty and therefore sees the meaning and truth of such an action as consisting only in the conviction that it (conscience) has about it.[32]

In order that everyone realize that any actions of conscience are not done arbitrarily or selfishly, such actions must be recognized as being grounded in the universal claim of duty and this is possible only if explicitly and publicly so stated. An individual can gain the necessary universal recognition of himself and his actions only if he expressly states that he is acting out of conviction. Only in *speaking out* are consciousness' existence and actions made known *(gewusst)* as the product of an individual certain *(gewiss)* of himself. This articulation, or speaking out, is the only way that an individual can effectively be recognized and understood by others.[33] In fact, consciousness enters the spiritual realm, having an adequate awareness of the nature of its existence *(Anundfürsichsein)*, only in speaking out and thus asserting its own individuality and subjectivity.[34]

Once again language, according to Hegel, is the immediate, actual manifestation of Spirit.[35] It serves as the means whereby

---

31 *Phänomenologie*, 445; Baillie, 644; Hypollite, II, 170. This self of conscience, Hegel continues, "is the *third self* that appears to us out of the third world of Spirit". *Ibid.* The other two "selves" (and their "worlds") were those of ethos and culture.

32 *Phänomenologie*, 450; Baillie, 651.

33 *Phänomenologie*, 458; Baillie, 660.

34 "Sehen wir auf die Sphäre zurück, mit der überhaupt die *geistige* Realität eintrat, so war es der Begriff, dass das Aussprechen der Individualität das Anundfürsich sei". *Phänomenologie*, 451; Baillie, 651.

35 "die Sprache [ist] das *Dasein* des Geistes als unmittelbaren Selbst..." *Phänomenologie*, 468; Baillie, 674.

one's own actions can be recognized and understood by others. By *saying* that "I" am acting out of conviction, I assert my own individuality and also gain an objective interpersonal status. Language is the existential form of Spirit in that through its use I create a social or universal self, to which I, as an individual, as well as others have a relation: "Language is self separating itself from itself".[36]

He therefore who says he acts so from conscience speaks the truth, for his conscience is the self as knowing and willing. But it is essential that he *say* so, for this self to be *universal* self as well.[37]

Thus though the self has immediately and individually asserted itself through speech, this speech is taken up, as we have seen before, as a mediating element *(Mitte)* whereby this individual is recognized by others as a public, moral self which is "universal". Each one knows his own conscience to be the essential factor in determining what is right or wrong. In articulating this conviction that one has acted from duty – from universal and not particular, selfish considerations, one endows one's individual actions with a significance with which other self-consciousnesses can identify. Concerning this expressed general significance, objectified as "universal self", "[the act] as such means nothing to it; what counts is the conviction that this act is a duty and this is effected [only] through language".[38]

---

[36] "Wir sehen hiermit wieder die *Sprache* als das Dasein des Geistes. Sie ist das *für andre* seiende Selbstbewusstsein, welches unmittelbar *als solches vorhanden* und als *dieses* allgemeines ist. Sie ist das sich von sich selbst abtrennende Selbst, das als reines Ich = Ich sich gegenständlich wird, in dieser Gegenständlichkeit sich ebenso als *dieses* Selbst erhält, wie es unmittelbar mit den andern zusammenfliesst und *ihr* Selbstbewusstsein ist..." *Phänomenologie*, 458; Baillie, 660-661.

[37] *Phänomenologie*, 460; Baillie, 663.

[38] *Phänomenologie*, 459; Baillie, 661; Hyppolite, 185.

F. FROM DUTY TO HYPOCRISY

In this discussion on the need for language in giving a proper moral perspective to individual actions, Hegel stresses the universalizing nature of linguistic statements, much as he had in other places, e.g., the section on "Sense-Certainty". Here, however, he is interested in examining the problem of the need for an individual to somehow *communicate* to others his intention to act out of duty. Intentions cannot be seen; they must be expressed and in so doing a network of relations between individuals is created and recognized. Language has provided the form for any moral act by formalizing and universalizing the framework and the intention upon which it is based. An individual becomes a moral agent only through this effectiveness of language.

The universality lies in the form of the action; it is this form which is effective *(wirklich)*. It is the *self* as such which is effective through language, which announces itself as the truth and through language recognizes all selves and is recognized by them.[39]

The language of conscience *(Gewissen)* is the language of consciousness certain *(gewiss)* of itself. This speaking out is the truth of any action and its only effective validation.

Consciousness expresses its conviction; in this conviction alone is the action duty: it holds good as duty, too, solely by the conviction being expressed.[40]

Through this verbalization of intention and duty, everyone is reciprocally recognized as acting conscientiously.[41] But because action receives its significance only from the words attached to its intent, people are not judged by what they *do,* but by what they *say;* duty becomes a matter of words and the expression of fine sentiments.

---

[39] *Phänomenologie*, 460; Baillie, 663.
[40] *Phänomenologie*, 459; Baillie, 661.
[41] "die Sprache, in der sich alle gegenseitig als gewissenhaft handelnd anerkennen..." *Phänomenologie*, 463; Baillie, 667.

Hegel, in one of his more ingenious dialectical turns, points up one of the consequences of a morality based upon the convinced and dutiful intention of the moral agent. Such a morality is predicated on the necessary gap between any particular action and the significance – universal or otherwise – ascribed to it. In Kantian terms, the very same action could be done from duty or from interest; only expressed formal conditions (i.e., the categorical imperative, etc.) can determine an action and therefore an agent's moral status. Unfortunately, such a situation where the determining factor of moral judgment is the formal, spoken intention behind it, leads to a state of hypocrisy *(Heuchelei)*.

The gap between the "universal" intention behind actions and the particular actions themselves (a characteristic condition of morality) can be transcended according to Hegel only by leaving the realm of finite existence and utilizing the categories present in religious thought and experience, categories based upon the self-consciousness of Absolute Spirit. Hegel's real attempt, however, at resolving the social and moral problems posed above, occurs in his *Grundlinien der Philosophie des Rechts*, where he demonstrates that only in the ethical life of the state can an individual act immediately and yet be assured that the springs of his action are grounded in his unmediated identification with the universal, absolute nature of the State.

G. CONCLUSION

Consciousness is propelled from one type of cognition to another by the felt disparity between its initial idea of its relation to and grasp of the outside world, and the truth which arises dialectically out of its attempt to express that idea. Hegel describes this process in detail in his Introduction to the *Phänomenologie*, where he determines the usage of many of his key notions. It is here that he gives his definition of experience as the dialectical movement whose efficient cause is the on-going incongruence between consciousness' initial cognition of an object and the actual implicit nature of that object, of which consciousness becomes explicitly aware as a different new object, which is the truth or experience of the former one.[42] A simple, but excellent example of this procedure is illustrated in Chapter III, where the given particular immediate object of sense-certainty becomes the mediated, universal qualities of perception.

Consciousness understands, rather than simply feels, this disparity between its supposed knowledge of its object and the object itself only when it attempts to *express* this knowledge. In attempting to verbalize the content of its experience, consciousness becomes aware of its dialectical nature. Furthermore, not only is language the most immediate and universal form of expression whereby consciousness gains an awareness of the meaning of its experience, but the dialectical implications of its meaning are explicitly present in the actual words which consciousness uses to describe it. Language is the *Dasein* of Spirit because this self-negating, yet self-correcting process is immanent in it. Consciousness can experience nothing unless it is brought to realize the gap between its apprehension of its world and that world as it truly is. Such a negating, self-alienating process, as Hegel calls it, is possible when consciousness realizes that the language it uses to describe its experience implicitly *(an sich)* conveys a better understanding of the dialectical quality of that experience than it hitherto has had for itself *(für sich)*. The *Bildung* of consciousness depends upon a continual realization on its part of the ability of language (and other forms of expression) to successfully reflect the inner inconsistency or dialectical nature of its own experiences. In this sense, I believe it is incorrect to say that language for Hegel is inadequate or limited in the *Phänomenologie*, as Ivan Soll has done in his recent

---

[42] "Diese *dialektische* Bewegung, welche das Bewusstsein an ihm selbst, sowohl an seinem Wissen als an seinem Gegenstände ausübt, *insofern ihm der neue wahre Gegenstand* daraus *entspringt*, ist eigentlich dasjenige, was *Erfahrung* genannt wird". *Phänomenologie*, 73; Baillie, 142. Like many key words and concepts in Hegel's philosophy, "experience" refers both to the *process* itself and the *result* of that process.

book on Hegel.[43] The fact that language does successfully express the experience of consciousness at any particular stage, revealing its inner dialectical nature, is an indication of its strength, not its weakness. To be sure, one language is superceded by another, rendering the first inadequate from a more advanced perspective, but, as W. M. Urban says of Hegel's notion of language,

this is a merely a step in a dialectic which finds *better words* for the expression of reality. The significant point is that *reality can be expressed*, that language is a vehicle for the exploration of the highest and deepest of the world.[44]

In our treatment of the role of language in Hegel's thought, we have thus far generally followed the order and content of the *Phänomenologie*. In the latter parts of the *Phänomenologie*, however, and in many of his later works, Hegel is no longer dealing with consciousness from the phenomenological perspective of its actual experiences in various "existential" situations. Language is no longer only characterized as the means for expressing the truth of the lived experience of consciousness, but possesses new qualities which reflect the more advanced stages of cognition which consciousness attains.

As we turn to examine the role of language in Art and Religion for Hegel and then finally and most importantly to the relation between language and absolute knowledge or philosophy, we cannot restrict ourselves to the *Phänomenologie*, but must range over all his works. This is necessary for several reasons. First, artistic production or religious experience cannot be understood primarily in terms of a subject-object or an intersubjective relationship such as those analyzed in the previous chapters. Art, Religion and Philosophy are in the domain of Absolute Spirit, because they are rationally realized products of man, conscious of his inner identity

---

[43] "An unsuccessful attempt to give linguistic expression to one of the forms of consciousness in the *Phenomenology* provides the necessary impetus for *progress* to a higher form. For Hegel, the limits of language are laudable". *An Introduction to Hegel's Metaphysics* (Chicago: University of Chicago Press, 1969), 102-103.

[44] *Language and Reality*. The Philosophy of Language and the Principles of Symbolism (New York: MacMillan, 1951), 30.

with the external world confronting him, and therefore are projections and objectifications of Spirit itself. Second, Hegel develops many of his original insights into art, religion and philosophy at great length in later substantial works, especially his posthumously published *Vorlesungen* on fine arts and religion and his two "Logics". His treatment of these topics in the *Phänomenologie* is rather limited, whereas he never again examines in such a fashion the epistemological, ethical and socio-cultural problems discussed above. Rather he uses the insights gained from the *Phänomenologie* as illustrations of his views, especially in his posthumously published *Vorlesungen* on the history of philosophy and the philosophy of history.

Finally, by turning to Hegel's later systematic works, we can come to some conclusion concerning his final views on language and the ultimate role it plays in the development of absolute knowledge or philosophy. In this connection it will be important to see what relationship exists between language as the expression or manifestation of Spirit *within* his philosophy (as stated in the *Phänomenologie*) and the expression of Spirit *as* philosophy and its language. In other words, is there a relation between Hegel's ideas on language and his use of philosophical language? The way Hegel uses language should illustrate and corroborate his actual views on the nature of language and its proper role in his philosophy.

PART III

LANGUAGE AND ABSOLUTE SPIRIT

VI

ART AND LANGUAGE

Self-consciousness enters the realm of Absolute Spirit when it becomes aware that its experience of alienation from the outside, object world has been transcended. It identifies itself as the source of the universal truths inherent in the natural, cultural and social world about it. Art, Religion and Philosophy are the means whereby self-consciousness expresses the nature of this identification and the knowledge arising from it. The first attempts at understanding and portraying the universal, rational nature of existence occur, according to Hegel, in art. Art is a productive activity which endeavors to create objects which will embody the particular universal truths which an individual or a community have experienced.

Hegel views art as a mode of religious expression; the artisan or artist is trying in various ways to express in physically concrete terms, a super-sensible reality (e.g., God or gods) which is the ground of all meaning and truth. In the *Phänomenologie des Geistes* and the *Enzyklopädie*, Hegel treats art only as a type of religious expression and points out the historical affinity between certain art-forms and certain types of religious consciousness. Art *qua* art (or in Hegel's words, the concept or *Begriff* of art) is dealt with only in his posthumously published lectures on the fine arts, *Vorlesungen über die Aesthetik*, in which we get a detailed treatment of the nature and history of artistic expression and productivity.

In this chapter, Hegel's treatment of art in the *Phänomenologie* will be examined first; it is here that the critical role of language is best seen. The section entitled *"Künstliche Religion"* could almost be called "Varieties of Religious Language". We shall then turn to portions of the *Propädeutik* and the *Enzyklopädie* which examine the psychological origins of language and intelligent expression in general and the nature of creative imagination *(Phantasie)* and the poetic process in particular. Finally, the relevant sections of the *Vorlesungen über die Aesthetik* on the origin and character of poetic language will be discussed so that Hegel's overall views on the role of language in the creative process can be clarified.

A. LANGUAGE AS THE ELEMENT FOR THE APPEARANCE OF THE DIVINE

In previous chapters we have seen the role that language plays as a medium for both initiating and revealing the dialectical process of human experience. Hegel's continued stress on language and the influence of the linguistic dimension in his description of the Art-Religions in the *Phänomenologie* is apparent. His discussion of the phenomenon and history of artistic creation is quite incomplete, and thus distorted, especially when viewed in the light of his later works. In the *Phänomenologie*, Hegel in effect confines himself to dealing with the linguistic forms of artistic expression. Man's increasingly successful attempts at depicting the divine in his creative forms of expression are illustrated by Hegel through the development of religious language and expression – from symbolic art to speculative propositions. His systematic treatment of the fine arts in his later lectures is in large part based upon the linguistic progression he adumbrates in the *Phänomenologie*.

As phenomenology or philosophy of religion, Hegel's approach is highly questionable. His lumping together of Judaism and Mohammedanism with all the oriental creeds as natural religions is tendentious, to say the least. The selectivity of fact and consequent distortion makes this analysis almost worthless. The primary redeeming feature is his description of the artistic element in Greek religion. His comments in this connection are worthwhile and reflect an attempt, later fully systematized, to organize and articulate the notion of a religion of art: a view commonly held by many German Romantics. His observations concerning the artistic dimensions of Greek religion and the religious aspects of Greek drama are penetrating.

Human consciousness goes through successive attempts at representing in sensible form that divine, super-sensible beyond with which it identifies its own self-conscious existence. Such representations progressively approximate consciousness' own conception of Absolute Spirit. Religious symbols and objects are initially produced by working over natural, physical objects and thus endowing them with a super-natural existence.

For what is consciously presented *(Vorgestellte)* only ceases to be something 'presented' and alien to spirit's knowledge, by the self having produced it, and so... the determination of the object as its *own* determination, and hence seeing itself in that object.[1]

Such religious art-symbols and art-objects (e.g., light, fire, animals) thus serve, according to Hegel, as projections of the knowledge thus far gained by consciousness. Initially such creations utilize the natural objects that are immediately present to consciousness. Gradually the worker or Artificer *(Werkmeister)* changes these natural objects into artificial ones, thus making them into hieroglyphs or symbols of certain non-natural ideas (e.g., half-human, half-animal, gods, etc.).

Eventually religious consciousness endows its representations of divinity with the ability to speak – only then adequately embodying the nature of self-consciousness. For Hegel, the *sine qua non* of selfhood and self-knowledge is the ability to speak, to externalize one's inner nature. The Artificer's pre-linguistic work

lacks the form and existence in which the self exists as self; it still fails to express in itself that enclosed within it is an inner meaning. It lacks language, the element wherein the in-dwelling significance is actualized.[2]

Without language – the *Dasein* of self as self, as self-expression – there can be no true recognition of oneself in one's productions, whether artistic, religious or philosophical. The dumb works of the

[1] *Phänomenologie*, 482; Baillie, 697. The nature and origin of this symbolizing process and its influence on Hegel's notion of dialectic have been described at length in Chapter II.
[2] *Phänomenologie*, 488; Baillie, 706; Hyppolite, II, 220.

Artificer in natural religion give way to the creative productions of the Artist, whose work is the expression of religion at the level of self-consciousness. The Artist interprets his experience of self-knowledge and self-recognition through human forms of expression, thus more adequately portraying the essence of self-consciousness or Spirit. Hegel calls the Artist a "spiritual worker" *(ein geistiger Arbeiter)*.

The work of art is now characterized by the nature of the language which the artist incorporates into his production. Initially such products are grounded in the immediate ethical spirit of a people (viz., the Greeks), and therefore are religious expressions of this concrete ethical unity. God first reveals himself in self-conscious form as Spirit in the language of a people. Language is "a way of existing which is immediately self-conscious".[3]

Hegel then outlines the development of various kinds of religious language as exemplified in the ancient Greek tradition. The first of these is the language of *immediate* self-consciousness; divinity is particularized and given the appearance of consciousness by being represented through an Oracle, which utters a language that can be immediately interpreted only in the light of the peculiar interests of the people, whose national Spirit it embodies.[4] Hegel contrasts this language of immediacy with the language of *mediated* self-consciousness: the Hymn. Through such expression, the individual participants experience a sense of community or universality and thus their language is the element in which their collective self-conscious Spirit, their God is manifested. God is present as creative expression, as a work of art animated with language.[5] Absolute Spirit receives its first true self-conscious existence through the language of religious communion, used by a people celebrating the presence of their God.

Eventually a pantheon arises where the various individual and

---

[3] "ein Dasein, das unmittelbar selbstbewusste Existenz ist". *Phänomenologie*, 496; Baillie, 716.

[4] *Phänomenologie*, 496; Baillie, 716.

[5] "Der Gott also, der die Sprache zum Elementes einer Gestalt hat, ist das an ihm selbst beseelte Kunstwerk…" *Phänomenologie*, 496; Baillie, 716.

national cults are represented in organic and collective fashion. The element and dwelling place of this pantheon, Hegel says, is language.[6] The ideas or images evoked by the linguistic arts (poetry, epic, drama) – collectively called the "Spiritual work of Art" – constitute man's ultimate attempt at expressing in graphic terms the nature of divinity and his relation to it.

Because language is the least corporeal mode of expression, it is best capable of representing man's inner thoughts and of reproducing his knowledge of the outer world. Language in general, especially the language of poetry and drama, can present a complete world of experience and is therefore much more suitable for portraying universal themes than those arts which rely upon visual or plastic media. Leading up to his discussion concerning the potentialities of such language, Hegel sums up the various kinds of religious expression hitherto described.

> The perfect element in which inwardness is as external as the externality is inward, is once again Language. But it is neither the language of the oracle, entirely contingent in its content and altogether individual in character; nor is it the emotional hymn sung in praise of a merely individual god; nor is it the meaningless stammer of delirious bacchantic revelry.[7]

Hegel proceeds to describe the various types of poetry and drama characterizing them according to the language employed. His classification is basically Aristotelian, i.e., the distinction between narrative or epic poetry and tragedy. However, he does think that comedy represents a "higher language" (Hegel's words) than tragedy. In the epic, the relation between the divine and the human is set forth in extended narrative form with a well-defined relationship and distance between ordinary man and the Olympian gods. The Epic *(Epos)* is pronounced by a minstrel *(Sänger)* who utilizes the natural language of his people. The minstrel merely serves as a channel, recalling in common speech, general episodes of his nation's historical existence. Hegel therefore likens him to

---

[6]   The various "*Volksgeister*" combine into a "Pantheon, dessen Element und Behausung [ist] die Sprache". *Phänomenologie*, 506; Baillie, 731.

[7]   *Phänomenologie*, 505; Baillie, 729.

Mnemosyne, the goddess of Memory or Recollection. The language of the minstrel is made up of externalized *Vorstellungen* – images or ideas – rather than universal concepts truly appropriate for fully expressing the nature of the divine. The *Vorstellungen* represent an interiorization and consequent expression of a common national experience.

In the "higher language" of Tragedy, the speaking individual is part of the drama itself, and does not exist apart from it, as did the minstrel singing his national epic. Therefore there is a closer relationship between the situation of the speaker and the language he uses. The language of the tragic hero expresses the pathos of the general human condition in the face of the alien world and the fate decreed by the gods. It exercises a universal appeal upon its audience. Various other types of language are spoken in the tragic drama, each of them articulating an aspect of human existence with which everyone can identify. Hegel talks of the language of the chorus of Elders, the voices of the gods, etc.

Finally, in Comedy, self-consciousness is represented as having mastered its destiny by overcoming its estrangement from a world controlled by the gods. The actors and the audience play themselves, for they now feel certain of themselves, their knowledge and their values. Such a people express their self-confidence through the language of Irony. It looks upon life with a sense of detachment, realizing that everything previously affecting it now has no real power over it.

Through the religion of Art, Spirit loses its external, alien form, its nature of being an object for a separate subject, and passes therefore, in Hegel's words "from the form of substance to that of subject".[8] Hegel sums up this process by analyzing a proposition that is first expressed in a comic vein, the final art-form mentioned.

In the Spirit which is completely certain of itself in the individuality of consciousness, all essential (distinctions) are submerged. The proposition which articulates this "lightmindedness" runs like this: *the Self is Absolute essential reality [das Selbst ist das absolute Wesen]*. The essential

---

[8] *Phänomenologie*, 521; Baillie, 750.

reality, which was substance and in which the self was accidental sinks to the level of a predicate and Spirit has in this self-consciousness, where nothing in the form of essential reality confronts it, lost its consciousness [of being a subject facing an object].[9]

The various types of language in the art-Religions described in the *Phänomenologie* serve as the perfect element for finally breaking down the distinction between subject and object, between experiencing consciousness and the world it initially confronts. This role of language is later deemphasized because Hegel's later works are written from a systematic, rather than a consciousness-oriented phenomenological point of view. Nevertheless, language for Hegel always serves as a means for mediating man's inner conscious world with the outer experienced one, as we shall see in his conception of the origin of language in sign-making imagination *(Zeichen machende Phantasie)* in the *Enzyklopädie*.

B. THE ORIGIN OF LANGUAGE: SIGN-MAKING *PHANTASIE*

In the various forms of creative imagination or *Phantasie* discussed by Hegel, the formal quality distinctive to all of them is their ability to evoke or represent the ideas to be communicated through pictorial means, either directly (symbolism, the visual and plastic arts) or indirectly (poetry). The highest form of expression for Hegel is what he calls sign-making imagination *(Zeichen machende Phantasie)*. The creation of signs by the productive memory *(produktives Gedächtnis)* represents the third and final type of intellectual activity (the other two being *Erinnerung* and *Einbildungs- kraft)* undertaken by man as a *vorstellendes Wesen*, as a being capable of ideally representing something to his own and other

---

[9] *Phänomenologie*, 521; Baillie, 750; Hyppolite, II, 258. In this citation, the transition from the comic language of art-Religion to what Hegel calls the "speculative propositions" of revealed religion is made apparent. Such "speculative propositions" as "The Self is Absolute reality", which form the core of Hegel's linguistic analysis of the next stage of Absolute Spirit – Revealed Religion – are examined at length in Chapter IX.

consciousnesses. Only in this type of *Phantasie*, are products created completely by and for the intellect. Alphabetical signs and constituted words exist and have meaning only through an arbitrary decision of what *Vorstellungen* they will represent. What letters or words look like (or, for the most part, sound like) has nothing to do with what they call to mind. The greater convenience and freedom of sign-making *Phantasie* over the other modes of ideative activity are apparent. One is no longer tied down to any particular object or its intuition as a vehicle for gaining knowledge. For Hegel, there may be natural symbols, but there are no natural signs.

As *designating (bezeichnend)* [activity], the intellect demonstrates thereby a freer choice and power in the use of intuitions than as [a] symbolizing [one].[10]

Hegel's discussion here is not particularly original, but his ambivalence toward poetic *Phantasie* is noteworthy. He groups the latter with the symbolizing and allegorical modes of *Phantasie*, but later, in the above citation, compares the superiority of signification to that of symbolization, rather than to its immediate predecessor, poetic *Phantasie*. Ultimately, Hegel does think that the ideas and truths expressed in art can be expressed in a higher form in religion or philosophy. But poetry, because it uses language, has a unique position among the arts. On the one hand it utilizes or evokes pictorial images and as such remains in the realm of art, while on the other, its external medium (i.e., words) does away with the necessity for any immediate physically present intuitions or objects.

In philosophical thinking, a word does not call up any image, but an abstract idea or *Vorstellung*.

The concrete idea is transformed through the *word-sign* into something altogether *imageless*, which is identified with the sign. (The image is extinguished and the word takes its place.)[11]

---

[10]   *Enzyklopädie* (1830), 458; *Hegel's Philosophy of Mind*, 213. Hegel's discussion of the sign-making process occurs in §§457-458 of the *Enzyklopädie*.
[11]   *Philosophische Propädeutik* (Stuttgart: Fr. Frommanns, 1929), § 159,

The language of poetry is like the language of abstract thought in that in both the immediate intuited world of sensation is done away with for consciousness.

Language is the extinction of the sensible world in its immediate [form of] existence, and its transformation into an existence which is an appeal that re-echoes in all ideating beings.[12]

Hegel's view of poetry is characterized primarily by his view of language. Though he certainly does not do justice to the aural and strikingly imagistic nature of much poetry, he by no means reduces it either to prose or pictorial fancy. As a form of cognition, Hegel grants a crucial role to the truths perceived and expressed in poetry. The *Vorstellungen* evoked by poetry express a higher truth than those naturally and immediately present to consciousness. Its language articulates the poet's awareness of the existence of ideal relations, beyond commonly sensed reality. The poet is a seer *(Seher)*, whose role is to make his readers "see" certain properties and qualities of existence of which they are unaware, or unable to experience themselves.[13] We now turn to the *Vorlesungen über die Ästhetik* in order to appreciate more fully Hegel's views on the role of language in artistic creation *per se* and the relevance of poetic language for his general philosophical purposes.

C. FORM AND CONTENT

Much of what Hegel says concerning language and poetry in these *Vorlesungen* is merely an elaboration and systematization of

---

pp. 210-211. The use of the *Propädeutik* rather than the relevant portions of the *Enzyklopädie* is intentional; the former's style – the book was meant as a teaching device – is much clearer and certainly more exoteric. Poetry is also specifically discussed in this work.

[12] *Philosophische Propädeutik*, 211.

[13] "Das Dichten ist nicht Nachahmen der Natur. Die Poesie ist in höherem Sinne wahr, als die gemeine Wirklichkeit. Der Dichter ist ein tiefer Geist, der die Substanz durchschauet, die ein Anderer auch in sich hat, aber die ihm nicht zum Bewusstsein kommt... der Dichter [ist] ein Seher..." *Philosophische Propädeutik*, § 154, p. 209.

remarks and ideas stated earlier in the *Phänomenologie* and his "Encyclopaedic" works. He repeatedly stresses the universal qualities present in language and its ability to communicate adequately the intellectual and self-conscious nature of human existence. "The word", Hegel says, "is able to express the whole of human spirit".[14] Hegel attributes much of the vaunted universal qualities of poetry to its linguistic medium, but makes it absolutely clear that language is the necessary external form for expression and that the ultimate artistic criterion resides in the quality of the *Vorstellung* which is then clothed in language through the imagination of the poet. The ideas expressed in poetry have been developed through the poetic *Phantasie* and then merely externalized in a medium – language – which was created solely by the mind for intellectual purposes.

In poetry, the *Vorstellungen*, proper to all spheres of art, are distilled from any immediate external form and presented mediately through words. The superiority of poetic imagination over other creative types of *Phantasie* lies in its ability to express its ideas without relying upon any sensuous materials. By freeing itself from any external material requirements, poetry captures the essential spiritual quality only implicitly resident in the other arts, and in creating its world, in effect repeats or recapitulates all previous modes of *Vorstellen*.

The proper medium of poetical representation is the poetical imagination and intellectual portrayal itself. And as this element is common to all types of art, it follows that poetry runs through them all and develops itself independently in each. Poetry is the universal art of the mind which has become free in its own nature, and which is not tied to find its realization in external sensuous matter, but expatiates exclusively in the inner space and inner time of the ideas and feelings.[15]

---

[14] *Vorlesungen über die Ästhetik III*, Vol. XIV of *Sämtliche Werke*, ed., Glockner (Stuttgart: Fr. Frommanns, 1939), 245. More specifically: "die Kunst der Rede, die Poesie überhaupt, [ist] die absolute wahrhafte Kunst des Geistes, und seiner Äusserung als Geist. Denn alles, was das Bewusstsein koncipirt und in seinem eigenen Innern geistig gestaltet, vermag allein die Rede aufzunehmen, auszudrücken und vor die Vorstellung zu bringen. Dem Inhalte nach ist deshalb die Poesie die reichste, unbeschränkteste Kunst". *Ästhetik I*, 260.

[15] *The Philosophy of Hegel*, ed. Friedrich (New York: Random House, 1954),

In turning to an examination of poetry and its medium, we shall therefore, in effect be dealing with the artistic element, *par excellence*.

Whenever Hegel is relating the function of art to his overall systematic endeavor at a philosophy of Spirit, the unique and particular qualities of its discipline get slighted. In its most extreme cases this takes the form of reducing artistic media – stone, paint, or language – to mere conventions, necessary only for externalizing what is already internally wholly created by the various modes of *Phantasie*. With poetry, this means that Hegel constantly refers to its medium as "mere symbols of speech" *(blosse Redezeichen)* which are themselves meaningless tones like all other signs. The process of *Vorstellen* is the crucial matter and artistic media appear to be mere channels, enabling an individual to undertake his own *vorstellendes* development.

The real objective form of inner life does not consist of sounds and words, but in my becoming aware of a thought, a feeling, etc., by making it into an object for consciousness and so having it ideally present to me... then developing for myself what is implicit in a thought or idea, setting forth external and internal relations of the content of my thoughts, relating the particular determinations one to the other.[16]

Poetry is considered superior to all other arts just because it creates formal means (signs and words) which have no significance in themselves, but exist and have value, however they are artistically handled, only in so far as they express an essential spiritual content.[17] Thus, "in art, as in all human works, it is the content which is ultimately decisive".[18] Its supreme function is to externalize, through adequate sensible means, something already completely worthy in itself. Philosophy of art, Hegel concludes, has as its

393-394; *Ästhetik I*, 131.

[16] *Ästhetik III*, 138. Unless otherwise noted, all translations are my own, although Osmaston's English translation has usually been consulted. *The Philosophy of Fine Art*, tr. F. P. B. Osmaston (London: G. Bell & Sons, 1920), III, 352.

[17] *Ästhetik II*, 260; Osmaston, III, 21.

[18] *Ästhetik II*, 240; Osmaston, II, 400.

chief concern the conceptualization of this content and the beautious ways in which it appears.[19]

It would seem that Hegel's attempt to emphasize the intellectual or spiritual content of Art would lead him to neglect or denigrate the formal requirements and characteristic elements of art in general, and individual artforms in particular. This criticism, however, levelled by many against Hegel, is in itself not that damning if his original systematic concerns are kept in mind. It does nevertheless undermine one facet of Hegel's philosophical position which is critical to his whole thinking: the separation of form from content. Such a separation leads to that very type of abstraction which he always disdained.

We have seen that one cannot separate the form from the content in any of the linguistic manifestations of Spirit hitherto discussed by Hegel in the *Phänomenologie*. Whether as the descriptive language of "Sense-Certainty" or "Perception", or the language of culture or morality, it has been shown that there is definite connection between the kind of language used and the nature of the experience or thought which it is reflecting or expressing. Hegel makes this same point in prefacing his remarks on the nature of poetic language, by stressing that the primary question is: what kind of *Vorstellung* must be adopted to assure appropriate poetic expression?[20]

The work of art is not "merely a sensuous thing, but Spirit manifested through a sensuous medium".[21] Elsewhere Hegel says of Spirit:

Spirit's mode of being is manifestation. Spirit is not some one mode or content whereof the utterance *(Äusserung)* and externality were a mere form distinct from it; Spirit does not reveal *something*, but its very mode of being and content is this revelation.[22]

---

[19] *Ästhetik II*, 240; Ostmaston, II, 400.
[20] "Den Ausgangspunkt für den gebildeten Ausdruck haben wir demnach in der gebildeten *Vorstellung* zu suchen, und unsere erste Frage auf die Form zu richten, welche das Vorstellen, um zu einem poetischen Ausdruck zu kommen annehmen muss". *Ästhetik III*, 274-275; Osmaston, IV, 57.
[21] *Ästhetik II*, 253; Osmaston, III, 15.
[22] *Enzyklopädie (1830)*, § 383, p. 314; *Hegel's Philosophy of Mind*, 16. The

This is especially true of the linguistic mode of expression, since "the art of speech, poetry in general, [is] the truly genuine art of the Spirit and its expression *(Äusserung)* as Spirit".[23] Poetic language embodies a certain *Weltanschauung*, and is capable of articulating certain qualities of experience that previous modes of expression, both artistic and non-artistic, cannot. What uniquely characterizes poetic language, endowing it with the universal capacity that Hegel claims for it?

D. IMMEDIACY AND POETIC EXPRESSION

It is best to begin with the origin of poetic language. For Hegel, like many others, including the German Romantics, poetry historically preceded prose and represented an original mode of cognition, where

the universal is not yet separated from its living existence in the individual (objects), law and phenomenon, ends and means are not yet contrasted with one another – and then once again rationalized together, but one is apprehended only in and through the other". [24]

Poetic *Vorstellung*, and therefore its language, initially reflected this primordial unity of universal and particular present in the mind of the poet. His vision and his words penetrated the sensuous curtain of ordinary experience, exposing and then expressing the essential universal qualities resident in the concrete objects immediately present to him. In contrast to common experience and understanding *(Verstand)*, which formulates categorical principles strictly on an inductive basis,

poetic intuition keeps the inner rationale *(Vernunft)* or reason of things together with its [external form of] expression and existence.[25]

---

translation of this passage, however, is from G. R. G. Mure, *A Study of Hegel's Logic* (Oxford: Clarendon Press, 1959), 296, n. 1.

[23]   *Ästhetik II*, 259-260; Osmaston, III, 21.
[24]   *Ästhetik III*, 239; Osmaston, IV, 22.
[25]   *Ästhetik III*, 241-242; Osmaston, IV, 24.

The apprehension and expression of this living immediacy of universal and particular does not take place *before* ordinary experience's facile categorization of the objects of sense-experience, but *after* it. In speaking of an original or even primordial living unity of experience, Hegel begins to sound like those intuitionists who claimed that true knowledge or at least true aesthetic experience (which is an essential factor in the cognition of truth) is found in the retention of that immediacy of experience present before the hard and fast categories of abstract thought and language are introduced and are consequently invoked as the standard for truth. The immediacy referred to by Hegel is however a mediated one, one that goes *beyond* the immediacy of sense-experience and then recaptures it in a way that lets its deeper meaning appear *(er-scheinen)*:

the actual image only presents the fact in its accompanying surroundings, whereas the expression of [poetic] imagination does not linger by the object in its immediacy, but proceeds to portray another image, through which the significance of the first should become clear and evident to us.[26]

Hegel continues by likening the figurative use of speech (metaphors, similes, imagery), the essential element of poetic representation, to a kind of covering *(Hülle)* which is not only ornamental, but also a classification or explanation of a definite aspect of the initially perceived content. Such imaginative creation attains a certain ideal objective status in our minds without being visibly or audibly externalized. A proper *Vorstellung* carries with it the possibility for its adequate expression, which may not actually be realized, but could be if necessary. "We always think in *words*", Hegel says, "without, however, thereby needing actual speech".[27]

Poetic imagination, in contradiction to immediate sensation or some form of primordial *aesthesis*, goes *beyond* the world of sense and its material objects and does not dwell *within* it. Therefore artistic creation is not merely the ability to reproduce or recall in purely physical terms some previous experience. It represents

---

[26]   *Ästhetik III*, 278; Osmaston, IV, 60.
[27]   *Ästhetik III*, 138; Osmaston, III, 352-353.

rather the conscious attempt at transcending the world of sense, not so much the desire to reproduce materially a certain object, event or feeling. Poetry epitomizes the creative endeavor in art of transcending the immediate sense-world and this is possible only through the nature of its medium: language. Poetry,

in its artistic embodiment is understandable essentially as the transcendence of actual sensation and its derogation [and] not as a production which simply has hitherto not been externally materialized....[28]

Hegel develops the theme, mentioned earlier in the *Phänomenologie* and the *Enzyklopädie*, that language (here, poetic) unites the universal and particular in a unique fashion. The "trick" in poetry is to create a particular image which carries with it definite intimations of a certain general or abstract idea. The strength of such language is its ability to transcend the limitations of particularity, and at the same time refer to a specific feeling, object or condition. This in-dwelling presence of the universal in a particular experience is possible only because certain words or poetic lines evoke and preserve a "cosmos" of their own. The intellectual or theoretical appeal of poetry (the worthiest type for Hegel) lies in its capacity to recreate an independent world, an organic whole where relations and qualities, freely posited and brought together, form in fact a work that seems anything but the product of license or random experience.[29] The vitality of such a creation lies in its expression of the universal, rational dimension in a self-contained unified whole whose language evokes the phenomenal "world" in which such a union can occur.[30]

E. POETIC LANGUAGE: REUNION OF UNIVERSAL AND PARTICULAR

The problem of understanding the nature of poetic language sharpens when one attempts to analyze its characteristic traits apart from

[28] *Ästhetik III*, 232; Osmaston, IV, 15.
[29] *Ästhetik III*, 229; Osmaston, IV, 12.
[30] *Ästhetik III*, 239; Osmaston, IV, 22.

its possible role as representing an original imaginative vision, which combines the universal and the particular into a living union. It is highly questionable whether poetry or song is indeed more ancient than prose. Poetry and song are more easily retained and memorized because of their rhythm and meter, but this does not preclude the possibility that narrative prose, though later forgotten, preceded them. Therefore the question as to what characterizes and differentiates poetic language from other artistic and linguistic forms of expression is the critical one, rather than the attempt at recapturing some sort of primal, lost language which will somehow reveal to us the meaning of human existence.

Hegel is aware of this when he states that we must distinguish between

a primordial poetry which existed before the cultivation of common artificial prose and the poetic conception and language which develops in the midst of a state of affairs which already possesses a finished prosaic form of expression.[31]

The problem confronting the poet in the latter situation, where he must somehow construct or reconstruct poetic language in opposition to the established common modes of thinking and speaking, is somehow to exhibit the special nature of his mode of *vorstellen*, separating it from existing prosaic ones.

Before comparing poetry to prose, let us examine the qualities which distinguish the poetic *Vorstellung* and its expression from other creative forms. The medium of language is superior to that of stone, tone or paint, primarily because of its extremely pliant or plastic *(bildsam, bildlich)* capabilities. Since words are mere signs that have been created by the intellect solely for expressing and conjuring up the realm of conscious experience, language is the best suited vehicle for mirroring the various complex qualities of the life of the Spirit.[32]

Poetic language presents a concrete image rather than an abstract idea, but does so in a way that evokes the universal or conceptual

---

[31] *Ästhetik III*, 240; Osmaston, IV, 21.
[32] *Ästhetik III*, 238; Osmaston, IV, 21.

categories which constitute the true definition or essential quality of the object or event portrayed. Such language is capable of expressing true *individuality*, something that other modes of expression are incapable of doing. Thinking is too abstract and the plastic and graphic arts are too beholden to the contingencies of a particular location in space and time. Poetry, Hegel says, "brings to us the concept in its *Dasein*, the generic in definitive individuality".[33]

Striking metaphors and picturesque adjectives used by Homer in describing the Greek gods or heroes and their exploits are among Hegel's favorite examples.[34] This is so because such imagery clothes the otherwise abstract significance which these actions have for explaining the motivations of human behavior. Such an approach has its literal uses as well, in the writing of history, for example. Proper historical explanation requires the ability to represent certain events in the personage and actions of an outstanding world-historical individual. Such individuals embody certain universal qualities and historical principles; a particular person comes to personify a certain general truth, thus putting flesh on an otherwise featureless abstraction, Hegel, in his section on poetic expression, uses the phrase "Alexander conquering the Persian empire" as a concrete illustration of the meaning of the world "victory".[35]

Another reason why language alone can capture true individuality, the general significance of a particular event or object, is its unique ability to portray the dynamic process of temporal development in an individual, or in the course of history. Quite often Hegel mentions this capacity of language to portray the dynamic course of spirit in phenomenal terms.[36] Only poetry,

---

[33] *Ästhetik III*, 277; Osmaston, IV, 58-59.
[34] For example, *Ästhetik III*, 278ff.; Osmaston, IV, 60ff.
[35] *Ästhetik III*, 277; Osmaston, IV, 59.
[36] For example: "[Concerning the sphere of Spirit] der als wirklicher erscheinender Geist erschöpfend nur kann dargestellt werden, wenn er uns als solch ein Verlauf vor die Vorstellung kommt". *Ästhetik III*, 224; Osmaston, IV, 7.

because of the nature of its linguistic medium, can express both
the process and individuality necessary to an adequately dynamic
and universal depiction of human existence. The visual arts are too
static and music too personal and non-representative. Poetic
imagination works in various ways to express its truths, consciously
seeking to differentiate itself from the ordinary language and
mentality about it.

The difference between the prose of ordinary consciousness and
the language of poetic imagination reflects for Hegel a difference in
outlook and cognition. He talks of poetic as opposed to prosaic
consciousness. What poetic consciousness does to separate itself
from prosaic life and thought is characterized by how it sets about
to articulate the vision it is trying to convey to its public.

Poetry has a philosophical purpose; its language and its appeal
result in the breaking down of ordinary static categories of understanding. In attempting to convey the dynamic nature of knowledge
and the universal import of particular human experiences – what
Hegel at one point calls "das individualisierte Vernünftige"[37] –
the language of poetry must resort to many devices. Among them,
the melting down of old modes of thinking and the re-coining of
novel ones through its usage of certain kinds of words and phrases
and figures of speech that are peculiar to poetry, or at least not in
common usage. Other ways of setting off the poetic from the prosaic
are the usage of different verbal orders, meter, rhythm and obsolete
words. In such cases ordinary thought patterns are broken down,
making the reader realize that the relation between subject and
object, universal and particular, sensible and non-sensible, is not a
static categorial one. Poetic language and poetic expression must
therefore undergo constant renewal and re-orientation, as previously
creative modes become part of matter of fact thinking and expression.

Hegel repeatedly makes it quite clear that the primary purpose
of art is to introduce a dynamic *Vernunft*-oriented cognitive mode
to replace the *Verstand*-oriented one of prosaic consciousness.

[37]   *Ästhetik III*, 244; Osmaston, IV, 27.

Poetic language and imagery serve as *the* means for effecting the transition from ordinary thinking to philosophv. Although the distinctive language of poetry is not to be identified with the speculative language of religion or philosophy, Hegel devotes much discussion to the implications that poetic expression have for acquainting individuals with the realm of dialectical reason and Spirit, and its consequent role in pointing towards a higher mode of thinking.

F. POETRY AS THE REVELATION OF THE DIVINE

Poetry breaks down common patterns of thought by converting prosaic modes of expression *(Ausdrucksweise)* into poetic ones.[38] It does this without resorting to any immediate, objective sensuous materials. Only in the poetic arts are actual, complete *Vorstellungen* involved. In detaching itself from all directly sensuous modes of representation, poetic *Phantasie* really transcends the general realm of art itself, which can be broadly defined as the "externalization in sensuous form of Spirit and natural objects".[39] Poetry does not rely upon sensed objects, but upon idealized mental objects which usually have pictorial or imagelike qualities.

While Hegel is intent upon marking out the boundaries of poetic expression, he admits that it is difficult to determine exactly where poetry ends and prose begins. A precise distinction between the common trivialities of ordinary language or the sharply delineated categories of understanding and the expression of poetic *Phantasie* is not always possible. However, poetic language must avoid leaving the sphere of imagination and its distinctive language for the higher intellectual forms of expression in religion and philosophy.[40] Nevertheless, poetry is that particular art from in which at the same time art itself begins to disintegrate, thus serving as the bridge

---

[38] *Ästhetik III*, 243; Osmaston, IV, 26.
[39] *Ästhetik III*, 220; Osmaston, IV, 3.
[40] *Ästhetik III*, 283-284; Osmaston, IV, 65.

to the religious mode of *Vorstellung* as well as the prose of philosophical thinking.[41]

Art, in poetic creation, carries within it the seed of its own destruction. As poesy gets further removed from concrete images, it becomes apparent that one can express the profounder universal knowledge of reason and self-consciousness without resorting to any sensuous representation at all. Furthermore, human consciousness is made to realize that it is indeed impossible to reconcile completely and harmoniously the truths of reason with the physical media or imaginative means at the disposal of the artist. Thus art at its highest level, poetry

> ...ends by transcending itself, inasmuch as it abandons the medium of a harmonious embodiment of mind in sensuous form, and passes from the poetry of imagination into the prose of thought.[42]

When in the history of human consciousness, art is no longer considered the highest fashion in which truth can obtain existence, art itself points beyond itself to the higher mode of thinking and expression: Religion.[43] Hegel nevertheless stresses the essential role of artistic expression in

> the liberation of Spirit from the substance and forms of finitude, ...the presence and reconciliation of the Absolute in the phenomenal sense-world [and] the unfolding of truth.[44]

Art, in Hegel's system, is the first part of Absolute Spirit and is on the same level as religion and philosophy. All "three realms... differ only in the *forms* through which they bring their object, the Absolute, into consciousness".[45]

Hegel continually identifies this Absolute Spirit with God and therefore sees the various art forms as the means whereby divinity is first actually and concretely represented. Poetry and drama,

---

41 *Ästhetik III*, 232; Osmaston, IV, 15.
42 *Ästhetik I*, 131; Friedrich, 394.
43 *Ästhetik I*, 150; Osmaston, I, 141.
44 *Ästhetik III*, 580; Osmaston, IV, 349.
45 *Ästhetik I*, 148; Osmaston, I, 139.

especially comedy (as mentioned in the first part of this chapter in our discussion on the *Phänomenologie*), constitute the final weaning away of consciousness from the need to appreciate the nature of its truth in an objective sensuous medium. The highest accomplishments of art are in the service of religion and philosophy and in fact represent a form of religion – *Kunstreligion* – as we have already seen in the *Phänomenologie*; through artistic imagination and expression Spirit and ultimately God himself as God is revealed. The nature of this revelation and its appropriate linguistic manifestation will be examined in the following chapters.

VII

THE SPOKEN WORD

The role of language as the means for transcending the various categorical distinctions of Understanding in Hegel's thought is fully appreciated when the notion of language as the *spoken* word, in religious terms, as the divine *Logos*, is explored. In examining the origins of Hegel's concept of *Logos*, his preference for the spoken word over the written one becomes apparent. In this connection, two critical ideas in his thinking will be analyzed: his concept of time and his rejection of mathematical or geometrical language and symbolism as incapable of reflecting adequately the higher order of rational conceptualization.

A. *LOGOS:* THE SPOKEN WORD

Hegel's preoccupation with religious themes as a means for expressing philosophical ideas is well-known. Hegel often invoked traditionally Christian ideas to break down the inflexible thought-patterns which he associated philosophically with the Kantian distinction between the phenomenal and noumenal world and, religiously, with the Old Testament religion of the Jews. Hegel's conception of the nature and role of language *vis-a-vis* philosophy was greatly influenced by the traditional Christian idea of *Logos* – the Word of God. Hegel's use of the *Word* (of God) as a means for explaining his ideas occurs throughout his writings. For example, Karl Rosenkranz recounts Hegel's intense desire – in his Jena-period lectures – to dissolve the fixed, dead categories which traditional theology used to describe the nature of God, His attributes and His relation to the World. In this connection,

Rosenkranz tells us that Hegel liked

> to represent the creation of the universe as the *uttering* of the absolute *Word*, and the return of the universe into itself as the *hearing* of the same, so that nature and history became a self-disappearing otherness between speaking and hearing.[1]

Hegel, in wanting to explain the nature of Absolute Spirit, finds in spoken language his perfect prototype. The dialectical character of the development of consciousness to absolute knowledge requires that Spirit (initially abstract, i.e., Logic) externalize or manifest itself thereby gaining knowledge of itself through another (i.e., the world of nature or history) and consequently returning to its original subject form as self-consciousness (i.e., Philosophy of Spirit). At the first stage in Hegel's thought, the logical development takes place *in vacuo.* Certain abstract relations are logically determined with the ultimate goal being the exhibition of an integral relationship between logical and natural or historical development. But initially the Logic requires an ethereal or supernatural medium whereby ideas can be articulated and communicated immediately and effortlessly without an external physical medium (*ein Anderssein* constituted of experienced natural objects or human events) which would only complicate the initial process of expression. Thus the appeal of spoken language to Hegel: a meaningful linguistic action externalizes or expresses something internal or abstract, which, once articulate, disappears, returning and referring to its source.

> The Logic represents the self-movement of the Absolute Idea only as the original *word*, which is an *expression:* an expression, however, which as external has immediately vanished again because it is. The self-determination... in which alone the Idea is, is *to hear itself speak....*[2]

---

[1]   *G. W. F. Hegels Leben*, p. 193.
[2]   *Wissenschaft der Logik, Zweiter Teil*, ed. Lasson (Leipzig: F. Meiner, 1948), 485. The above translation is taken (except for the italics which follow the German text) from *Hegel's Science of Logic*, tr. Johnston & Struthers (New York: Macmillan, 1929), II, 467; see also *Hegel's Science of Logic*, tr. A. V. Miller (London: Allen & Unwin, 1969), 825.

Language represents one way consciousness can express or project itself from *within* itself, yet still gain objectivity.

The best introduction to an understanding of Hegel's notion of *Logos* is the discussion of Jakob Boehme in his *Geschichte der Philosophie*. Hegel greatly admired such German mystics as Boehme, whom he considered the first representative of German philosophy, primarily because of his ability to combine apparently contradictory or contrary qualities or ideas into meaningful expressions. Hegel's ideal of a philosophical terminology which would adequately mirror the dialectical nature of experience was greatly influenced by the language of German mystics like Boehme, although from a philosophical standpoint, he viewed the latter as a "barbarian".

Hegel outlines Boehme's view of the *Word* as revelation and separation from God. Something becomes manifestly known, in general, only with its becoming objectively present to the knower, an object for a subject. Even God can only know Himself, says Boehme, if He externalizes Himself. This externalization is the Word of God which Hegel parenthetically identifies with the Son, the second member of the Trinity. "The Word is the efflux of the divine One, and yet God Himself as His revelation".[3]

At this point Hegel comments on Boehme's use of the word "*Wort*", saying:

Λόγος is more definite than word, and there is a delightful double significance in the Greek expression indicating as it does both reason and speech. For speech is the pure existence of spirit; it is a thing which when once heard goes back within itself.[4]

Hegel obviously finds the dual meaning of *Logos* quite congenial to his purposes. God reveals himself through his words; He be-

---

At one point Hegel talks of one of the individual manifestations of Spirit "...als die reine Sprache oder das Werden der Gestalt, deren Dasein nicht aus dem Selbst heraustritt, und rein *verschwindender* Gegenstand ist"; *Phänomenologie*, 525; Baillie, 754.

[3] *Geschichte der Philosophie III*, 314; Haldane, *Lectures on the History of Philosophy*, III, 204.

[4] Haldane, *Lectures* III, 204.

comes the Word or *Logos*, and in so doing makes manifest the rational nature of Spirit.[5] In identifying Reason *(Vernunft)* with *Logos*, the self-transcending nature of language as God's language or revelation, is once again stressed. In almost every passage where *Logos* as reason or the divine Word is cited by Hegel, he is sure to mention its capacity for disappearing by being heard or taken up once again, thus playing on the words *Vernunft* and *Vernehmen*. That which is purely rational – *Logos* – gets taken up immediately, thus transcending itself in proper dialectical fashion. This self-transcending quality of God's word and work allows Hegel to interpret the third verse of the first chapter of *Genesis* ("And God said, 'Let there be light'. And there was light.") as expressing the ultimate self-negating and self-transcending of Divine creation and expression.

Here we have one of the sublimest passages. The Word represents the greatest possible absence of effort and this breathing is here at the same time light, the world of light, the infinite pouring forth of light and thus light is degraded to the rank of a word, to something so transitory as a word.[6]

Hegel's intentness upon stressing the evanescent nature of the products of Divine revelation would seem to deny the ultimate existence of the second person of the Trinity. But, typically, Hegel sees in this self-negating process the very essence of God. The Divine can only be understood as this continual, infinite transcending of all rational means of mediation and expression. The nature of spoken language, *Logos*, best expresses this quality of evanescence, yet ultimate permanence.[7]

---

[5]   "Gott ist Schöpfer und zwar in der Bestimmung des *Logos*, als das sich äussernde, aussprechende Wort..." *Vorlesungen über die Philosophie der Religion II*, Vol. XVI of *Sämtliche Werke*, ed. Glockner (Stuttgart: Fr. Frommanns, 1928), 245; *Lectures on the Philosophy of Religion*, ed. & tr. E. B. Speirs & J. B. Sanderson (London: Kegan Paul, Trench, Trübner and Co., 1895), III, 31.

[6]   *Philosophie der Religion II*, 62; *Philosophy of Religion*, II, 188.

[7]   In talking of the intrinsically perishable nature of all mediating forms, Hegel says, "Die Sprache vereinigt... die Bedeutung dieses *Untergangs* und des *Grundes;* man sagt, das Wesen Gottes sei der *Abgrund* für die endliche Vernunft".

God Himself, or the Absolute as Spirit, is ultimately revealed as a dynamic process of self-articulation and self-abnegation. "This movement itself", Hegel says, "expresses the absolute Being as *Spirit*".[8] This last statement points to another implication of Hegel's use of the model of spoken language for explaining the experience and expression of ultimate truth in its rational *(Vernünftige)* form. The flexible, non-categorical nature of experience is brought home by emphasizing the transitory nature of the spoken word; the activity of spoken language serves as the paradigm for the self-transcending activity of Spirit.

It is the Word, which pronounced, externalizes and empties him who pronounces it, but which is nevertheless taken up immediately, and only in this taking up of itself does the Word exist. Thus, the differences which are made, are just as immediately dissolved, as they are made, and just as immediately made as they are dissolved; truth and reality are precisely this self-circular movement.[9]

By breaking down any hard and fast categories, whether psychological (subject and object) or metaphysical (form and content), consciousness is able to reconcile conflicting extremes.

In the *Phänomenologie*, the religious language of reconciliation serves as the vehicle for the first revelation of Absolute Spirit itself to consciousness. At the end of the section on "Evil and Forgiveness" *("das Böse und seine Verzeihung")*, two extreme forms of ethical consciousness are reconciled through the spoken word. Hegel finds in the confessional language of mutually forgiving individuals the first actual manifestation of the recognition of oneself in others and consequent identification with them. This condition uniquely characterizes the realm of Absolute Spirit for Hegel.[10] Hegel makes two points here; first that in the very language

Wissenschaft der Logik, Zweiter Teil, 104; Struthers & Johnston, II, III; Miller, 483.

[8] *Phänomenologie*, 535; Baillie, 767.
[9] *Phänomenologie*, 534-535; Baillie, 767; Hyppolite, II, 274.
[10] "Das Wort der Versöhnung ist der *daseinde* Geist, der das reine Wissen seiner selbst als *allgemeinen* Wesens in seinem Gegenteile, in dem reinen Wissen seiner als der absolut in sich seienden *Einzelheit* anschaut, – ein gegenseitiges Anerkennen, welches der *absolute* Geist ist". *Phänomenologie*, 471; Baillie, 677.

of reconciliation there occurs a theophany, an appearance of the Divine itself. He concludes the lengthy 160-page section on Spirit in the *Phänomenologie*, "The reconciling *Yes* ...[is] God showing Himself in the midst of those who know themselves as in pure knowledge".[11] Second, this language is a *spoken one* – one of commitment and affirmation in a concrete social and ethical situation. "Yes", or "I am so" *("Ich bin's")* are *spoken* words, gaining meaning only in a specific context. Hegel later says that Spirit is truly understood as the process in the course of which "absolute opposites are recognized as identical and this recognition breaks forth as the *Yes* between these extremes".[12]

B. CONSCIOUSNESS, SPACE AND TIME

The self-transcending nature of spoken language which Hegel sees as embodying and expressing the very activity of God, Absolute Spirit or Subject, is related to another important aspect of his thought: his conception of time.

Speech has always been regarded as a manifestation of God, because it is not corporeal; as sound it is temporal and immediately disappears; its existence is therefore immaterial.[13]

The appeal to spoken language as the best vehicle for revealing the nature and development of self-consciousness as Spirit is based upon its quality of being meaningful, yet momentary. Playing upon the evanescent yet durational aspects of time, Hegel says it is "Being, which while it *is*, is *not*, and while it is *not*, it *is*".[14] Hegel describes the dialectical relationship of these apparently contradictory qualities of time as follows:

---

11 *Phänomenologie*, 472; Baillie, 679.
12 *Phänomenologie*, 547; Baillie, 782-783; Hyppolite, II, 288.
13 *Geschichte der Philosophie I*, 24; *Lectures on the History of Philosophy*, I, 392.
14 *Enzyklopädie* (1830), §258, p. 209; *Hegels Philosophy of Nature*, tr. A. V. Miller (Oxford: Clarendon Press, 1970), 34.

Time is an absolute passing-beyond-self, a creation of the One (the point of time or Now), which immediately becomes the annihilation of it, and also the perpetual annihilation of this destruction; so that this self-creation of Not-being is also simple self-equality and self-identity.[15]

Time and the paradoxical formulations of its character have fascinated philosophers since Zeno and Heraclitus. Of interest to us, however, is the role it plays in Hegel's description of the experience of self-consciousness.

Spoken language gains its spiritual, ideal qualities because it occurs in time which is the ground of the restless self-negating yet self-sustaining quality of all experience.[16] We have already seen in Chapter II how Hegel, influenced by the early Romantic tradition, claimed primacy for the sense of hearing over the sense of sight. Hegel often discusses the temporal nature of sound or tone, the purely physical basis of speech. As sounds or tones, spoken words diappear in time as quickly as they are uttered, leaving their meaning implanted in the listener, in an ideal yet fluid form. Hegel's idea of time, and consequently sounded speech, can be understood only if it is seen in the light of its role as the means for transcending the sharp distinction of our visual and spatial world. Hegel sees spatial characteristics as reflecting the static categorical nature of Understanding, while time directly embodies the fluid self-transcending nature of thinking itself.[17] In the last pages of the *Phänomenologie* Hegel stresses the dual character of time as the immediate intuited form of thinking itself as well as its ultimate *Aufhebung* in Absolute Knowledge.[18]

---

[15] *Wissenschaft der Logik, Erster Teil*, 182; Struthers & Johnston, I, 203; Miller, 189.

[16] "Die Zeit ist das Negative im Sinnlichen." *Philosophie der Geschichte*, Vol. XI of *Sämtliche Werke*, ed. Glockner, 117. Also, "die Zeit ist nun eben das Dasein dieses beständigen Sich-Aufhebens..." *System der Philosophie, Zweiter Teil: Die Naturphilosophie*, Vol. IX of *Sämtliche Werke*, Zusatz to §257, p. 78; *Hegel's Philosophy of Nature*, 34.

[17] "die Zeit... ist der daseinde Begriff selbst..." *Phänomenologie*, 38; Baillie, 104.

[18] "Die *Zeit* ist der *Begriff* selbst, der *da ist*, und als leere Anschauung sich dem Bewusstsein vorstellt; deswegen erscheint der Geist notwendig in der Zeit, und er erscheint so lange in der Zeit, als er nicht seinen reinen Begriff *erfasst*,

What is of specific concern to us, however, is the essential role of time in explaining the nature of the conscious process of the ego itself, and, in this regard, the relation between time and space. Hegel often sees the temporal process as the best way of expressing the activity of self-consciousness. When the particular contents of consciousness are abstracted, we are left with an awareness of the underlying nature of the knowing process itself as constant self-expression and its consequent self-absorption. Such a movement represents the motion of time itself.

Ego is in time and time is the being of the conscious subject itself. Inasmuch, then, as time and not the spatial condition as such supplies the essential element... for this reason tone... penetrates into the self of conscious life, seizes hold of the same in virtue of the most simple aspect of its existence and places the ego in movement by means of the motion in time and its rhythm.[19]

The temporality of sound or music conveys the distinctive nature of the inner life of the conscious knowing subject.[20] Hegel also contrasts the dynamic negating quality of sounded tones in time with the static, quantitative characteristics of space. Rightly or wrongly, he sees in the experience of temporality a closer approximation to the ultimately fluid non-material nature of reality. Space is the intuitional form of Understanding, while time is the intuitional form of Reason. Therefore, just as the hard and fast categories of Understanding find their ultimate justification and fulfillment in the process of Reason, so the discrete, purely quantitative distinctions of space find their dynamic resolution in the dimension of time. "The truth of space is time".[21]

---

d.h., nicht die Zeit tilgt. Sie ist das *äussere* angeschaute Begriff; indem dieser sich selbst erfasst, hebt er seine Zeitform auf, begreift das Anschauen, und ist begriffenes und begreifendes Anschauen". *Phänomenologie*, 558; Baillie, 800.
[19] *Ästhetik III*, 151; Osmaston, III, 365.
[20] "denn der Ton, indem er nur durch das Negativgesetztsein der räumlichen Materie sein ideelleres zeitliches Dasein gewinnt, entspricht dem Innern, das sich selbst seiner subjektiven Innerlichkeit nach als *Empfindung* erfasst..." *Ästhetik III*, 7; Osmaston, III, 221–222.
[21] *System der Philosophie. Zweiter Teil*, Zusatz to §257, 79; *Hegel's Philosophy of Nature*, 34.

This necessary transition from the world of space to the world of time is described from the artistic standpoint when Hegel examines the development of the aural/oral arts out of the visual ones. Music, and later poetry, because of the temporal nature of their medium, reflect more profoundly the qualities of subjectivity and the idealization and transcendence of the sensuous world. The unique experience of a conscious, knowing subject as well as the *vorstellende* idealizing process of knowledge are more adequately portrayed when the purely quantitative, qualitatively indifferent spatial plotting of expression gives way to the interpenetrating sensuous-negating power of music and language. Such forms of expression concentrate themselves into single, transitory moments of time rather than physically permanent structures and, therefore, gain their real existence only in the stream of memory and the interrelating power of consciousness. Such modes of expression and the manner of their apprehension reflect much more closely the dynamic, idealizing process of human consciousness.[22]

Hegel exhibits his prejudice against mathematical knowledge quite frequently in his writings; his primary objection is that the quantitative nature of mathematics and the spatial world of geometry cannot grasp the qualitative dynamic relations that must be articulated and worked out in speculative thinking. The world of numbers and geometrical figures deals only in superficial, external relations among objects and events and never comes to grips with internal relations; it is therefore unable to explain the connection and dialectical development of various ideas or experiences of

[22] Hegel explains this transition from the use of a spatially oriented form of expression in painting to a temporally-oriented form in music when describing the specific nature of the media and the material used by the latter.

"Ihr Material, obschon noch sinnlich, geht zu noch tieferer Subjektivität und Besonderung fort. Das Ideellsetzen des Sinnlichen durch die Musik besteht nämlich darin, das gleichgültig Auseinander des Raumes... nun gleichfalls aufzuheben und in das individuelle Eins des Punktes zu idealisiren... Solche beginnende Idealität der Materie, die nicht mehr als räumlich, sondern als zeitliche Idealität erscheint, ist der Ton, das negative gesetzte Sinnliche, dessen abstrakte Sichtbarkeit sich zur Hörbarkeit umgewandelt hat, in dem der Ton das Ideele gleichsam aus seiner Befangenheit im Materiellen loslöst". *Ästhetik I*, 129; Friedrich, 391-392.

consciousness. Hegel thought mathematics defective because it could neither portray the dynamic nature of the knowing process nor make meaningful distinctions between various qualities resident in our experiences. His best known attack on the reductionist, purely quantifiable, nature of mathematics and its application to a spatial medium occurs in his Preface to the *Phänomenologie*.

Space is the existence into which the Concept writes its distinctions as into an empty, dead element in which they are equally immobile and lifeless. The actual is not something spatial the way it is considered in mathematics.[23]

C. ALPHABETICAL VS. SIGN LANGUAGES

Hegel's anti-scientific bias (science being defined here collectively as those disciplines whose sole or primary purpose lies in the strict quantification of their subject matter), typical of many 19th-century continental thinkers (e.g., Schopenhauer), is of importance to us only in so far as it helps to explain his attitude toward the languages of mathematics and science in general and, more specifically, his objections to the development of a formal logic as a worthwhile philosophical instrument. Most of Hegel's comments along this line are found in § 459 of the *Enzyklopädie*, where he discusses the advantages and defects of various types of linguistic expression. In this section his immediate concern is an analysis of the relative merits of sign, as opposed to alphabetical, languages. In the process, however, he injects various considerations concerning spoken (sounded in time) versus written (transcribed in space) language. Several related matters that have been dealt with in this chapter are drawn together by Hegel, and certain interesting

---

[23] *Phänomenologie*, 37. The English translation is from Kaufmann, *Hegel*, 420. Later Hegel discusses the "paralyzed" nature of such quantified knowledge. "Das Prinzip der *Grösse*, des begrifflosen Unterschiedes, und das Prinzip der Gleichheit, der abstrakten unlebendigen Einheit, vermag es nicht, sich mit jener reinen Unruhe des Lebens und absoluten Unterscheidung zu befassen". *Phänomenologie*, 38-39; Baillie, 104.

implications for his conception of language and philosophy can be drawn.

In Chapter II where we traced the origin of Hegel's concept of symbol and sign, we noted that the process of signification – of an object or representation being given another meaning (other than its own immediate, natural significance) by and for consciousness – embodied *par excellence* the transcending, yet preserving *(aufhebende)* quality of the experience of consciousness. Hegel begins § 459 by noting that signs *qua* signs exist only as *aufgehobene*, as a given in space whose original meaning has been negated by consciousness. He continues by noting that the true self-transcending quality which a sign has for the intellect is better seen when it is given an ideal existence through a sounded, temporal sign which disappears as soon as it is.[24]

Hegel then comments on the various types of written language. He prefaces his remarks by noting that

Language comes into consideration here only in its characteristic form as the product of the intellect, manifesting its representations in an external medium.[25]

Hegel is not interested in what he calls the "anthropological" or "psycho-physiological" aspects of speech and its origins, but rather in the nature and relative merits of the various ways in which the content of language is systematically represented and retained. Vocal, rather than written, language is primary, both chronologically and philosophically, since the former relies upon the *temporal* nature of sound, while the latter is based upon *spatial* configurations. Hegel defends at length an ordinary alphabetical language, as opposed to a formal type of sign-language, in which each simple

---

[24] "Die Anschauung, als unmittelbar zunächst ein Gegebens und Räumliches, erhält, insofern sie zu einem Zeichen gebraucht wird, die wesentliche Bestimmung, nur als aufgehobene zu sein. Die Intelligenz ist diese ihre Negativität; so ist die wahrhaftere Gestalt der Anschauung, die ein Zeichen ist, ein Dasein in der *Zeit*, – ein Verschwinden des Daseins, indem es ist... der *Ton*, die erfüllte Äusserung der sich kundgebenden Innerlichkeit". G. W. F. Hegel, *Enzyklopädie (1830)*, 369; *Hegel's Philosophy of Mind*, 213-214.
[25] *Enzyklopädie (1830)*, 370; *Hegel's Philosophy of Mind*, 214.

idea would be represented by a simple sign. The individual signs of such a language would seem to be more precise than individual words in a natural language. Furthermore, once certain ideas are established, it would make international communication possible, since each idea would have a sign that was not dependent upon the vagaries of ordinary language and the dangers of mistranslation.

Hegel called such a formal language a hieroglyphic one, since it used simple signs or figures to represent (sometimes even with pictorial similarity) simple ideas. Such a language presupposes an atomistic view of reality and thought. It assumes that one can analytically reduce the various *Vorstellungen* and abstract thoughts present to consciousness to logical, non-composite terms, without thereby doing violence to the ordinarily composite, interrelated nature of such mental constructs.[26]

Hegel claims that such an analytic, atomistic approach to the problem of human expression fails to recognize the basic role of language as a system of conventional, in themselves meaningless, signs, i.e., names, designed to refer as pointers to certain mental objects which are being entertained or communicated. The true role of language is to present as directly and immediately as possible the various mental intuitions and constructs present to consciousness. Therefore, Hegel thought that such an analytical approach resulted in individual signs being viewed as definitions and (pictorial) representations rather than as arbitrary signs conveying their meanings only when synthesized with the actual experience of the speaker or auditor. With this goal in mind, the necessary qualities for a language are ideally present in its spoken form and next best, in its alphabetical form, viz., having those characteristics which stress that language serves only as an external medium which immediately points beyond itself to a non-sensuous

[26] "Die Hieroglyphensprache entsteht... aus der voranzugehenden Analyse der Vorstellungen, woraus dann leicht der Gedanke gefasst wird, dass alle Vorstellungen auf ihre Elemente, auf die einfachen logischen Bestimmungen zurückgeführt werden könnten, so dass aus den hierfür gewählten Elementarzeichen... durch ihre Zusammensetzung die Hieroglyphensprache erzeugt würde". *Enzyklopädie* (1830), 372; *Hegels Philosophy of Mind*, 217.

universal world of meaning. The flux of experience and the dialectical nature of knowledge require that such signs or names be
understood as pointing to notions or ideas that are not static,
but have various levels of meaning, at times apparently contradictory to one another.

Attempts to construct a formal language suffer the same dis-
advantages which Hegel attributes to the languages of mathematics
and geometry. Such means of expression are fine and necessary on
a certain level – that of the Understanding – but they cannot hope
to have a speculative purpose, i.e., reveal the higher rational nature
of experience and existence. For this purpose we must rely upon
language as the means for simply and directly bringing to mind the
various *Vorstellungen* which the knowing, conscious activity red-
integrates according to its own level of experience and knowledge.
Even when our ideas are "broken down" and analyzed into a
composite of symbols and signs, thinking organically relates them
to a concrete, specific context, and re-unites them into a single
thought.[27]

D. LANGUAGE AS A SPECULATIVE INSTRUMENT

In an alphabetical language, the ultimate purpose of a language as
an intrinsically self-transcending (both temporally and spatially,
since the vocal signs and their configurations have no meaning, but
simply point beyond themselves) system of names is most apparent;
it also allows for the widest range of expression. It enables consciousness to express itself in a medium which does not formalize
and rigidify its relationship to the external world it is meant to
describe.

Hegel's conception of language, especially as noted in § 459 of
the *Enzyklopädie* is obviously worthless to someone who thinks

[27] "das Denken resumiert den konkreten Inhalt aus der Analyse, in welcher
derselbe zu einer Verbindung vieler Bestimmungen geworden, in die Form
eines einfachen Gedankens". *Enzyklopädie (1830)*, 373; *Hegel's Philosophy of
Mind*, 217.

that the primary purpose of language is to remove all possible vagueness and equivocality by narrowing down and analyzing all ordinary terms of speech into a form, artificial or otherwise, which would allow for the univocal designation and expression of particular ideas or images and their respective components. It should be just as obvious, however, that for Hegel the purpose of language as a philosophical tool is to reflect such equivocality and flexibility of meaning and expression. Formalistic approaches to the use and creation of language have important functions to perform, but are useless for pointing out the universal, internally related, dialectical qualities of experience, which give the sense-world its true meaning and for which reason Hegel saw language as the manifestation of the realm of Spirit.

In a thoroughly arbitrary mode of writing, such as an alphabetical one, Hegel says that the visible (i.e., written in space) stands in proper relation to the audible (i.e., spoken in time), because the "visible language relates itself to the sounded one only as a sign, [for] the intellect expresses itself immediately and unconditionally through speaking".[28] Hegel's concept of language is based in large part on the qualities resident in language as a spoken, temporal medium. In the next chapter we shall examine his views as to what specific content or construction *in* a language best lend themselves to philosophical thinking and how they give us guidelines for comprehending the world of Absolute Knowledge.

[28]   *Enzyklopädie (1830)*, 374; *Hegel's Philosophy of Mind*, 218.

VIII

THE SPECULATIVE POWERS OF LANGUAGE

In the preceding chapters we have traced Hegel's thoughts on the role of language as an expressive medium. We have dwelt primarily upon the ability of language to act as a vehicle for the articulation of various conditions of experience and states of knowledge in which consciousness finds itself. Language embodies the static categories of understanding necessary for the initial learning process, but points as well to a more fluid type of knowledge. It acts as the mediating mechanism between initially abstract universal concepts and the brute particulars of immediate experience. Language itself expresses in various ways the universalizing process which consciousness must undergo to attain philosophical awareness. The spoken word, discussed in the last chapter, perhaps embodies most vividly the role of language in expressing the dialectical nature of reality.

Up to this point we have stressed primarily the formal role of language in general as an expressive medium. Little has been said about Hegel's relationship to the specific content *within* language and its role, if any, in explaining or expressing the dynamic dimension of experience. Such an investigation will expose certain assumptions concerning Hegel's ideas on language which will be of great help in coming to any final conclusions concerning his positions on the relationship between philosophy and language.

Whenever Hegel analyzes the meaning or content of any word or statement, he usually refers specifically to such words, phrases or sentences which occur in ordinary, natural language, in universally applicable situations. When he examines more esoteric or mystical formulations, he consistently does so with a view to relating them to the more exoteric experiences of consciousness. Also, since

Hegel uses examples of ordinary language, arising out of concrete common human experience, any speculative dimension or implications which such language may have would be lost, at least initially, on the naive consciousness uttering it. Such a condition has two further implications. First, a true appreciation of the deeper philosophical or speculative dimension of natural language can dawn upon human consciousness only when it has itself gone through various stages of experience and fully digested their meaning and implication, as occurred, for example, in the *Phäno-menologie*. Second, the full irony of man's use of language becomes apparent – naive consciousness, in its own common language, is articulating ideas which it never learned or thought of.

Language, as Hegel often states, is the manifestation of Spirit; it is *Logos*, revealing the inner rational structure of experience and reality. If linguistic formulation is to be viewed as the closest approximation in ordinary experience to the dialectical process inherent in the cognitive processes of consciousness, and if therefore language itself constitutes an incipient "logic of process" which captures truth in its fully developing forms, then the actual, specific words and constructions used by consciousness should reflect the dialectical conditions of knowledge.

This ability of consciousness to express in its ordinary language, unself-consciously *(bewusstlos)*, the active dialectical quality present in all forms of human experience constitutes its speculative power. Hegel's references to and manipulation of the various meanings and implications of certain words and grammatical constructions of ordinary language in general, and German in particular, exemplify his belief that expressions in language can point towards the higher truths of reason and the realm of self-conscious Spirit. In this chapter we shall examine three different aspects of the speculative nature of language as treated or touched upon by Hegel. First, his constant references to or usage of puns, etymologies and common linguistic usage; then, his theory of judgment with specific reference to his notion of the "Speculative Proposition"; and finally his views on the adequacy or inadequacy of religious thought and language.

Hegel uses the word "speculative" in describing all three of these types of expression, and gives this word a definite meaning. "Speculative" refers to that quality in knowledge, language or experience which points out and expresses its dialectical, fluid nature. For example, it refers to the overcoming of any hard and fast distinctions between the subject and object in experience (and in a related fashion, the subject and predicate in grammatical forms) as in the "journey" of consciousness in the *Phänomenologie*. The speculative, Hegel says, "expressly rises above such oppositions as that between subjective and objective, which the understanding cannot get over, and absorbing them in itself, evinces its own concrete and all-embracing nature".[1] Such *speculative knowledge* therefore also involves rising above the "either/or" values and judgments of traditional logic, or as Hegel puts it, it consists "in the comprehension of the Unity of Opposites, or of the Positive in the Negative".[2]

It is this ability to see the speculative, to see different – or better, contrary or contradictory – meanings in a simple word or sentence, that Hegel seeks to develop and encourage. In so doing, the mind will be prepared for understanding the dialectical nature of true knowledge itself. Hegel emphasizes that the tension of contrary meanings and seemingly contradictory judgments must be retained in speculative thinking; they should not be translated into or reduced to set, univocal formulae or dismissed as meaningless.

Speculative thought consists only in this, that thought hold fast Contradiction, and in Contradiction, itself, and not in that it allows itself to be dominated by it – as happens to imagination – or suffers its determinations to be resolved into others, or into Nothing.[3]

---

[1]   *System der Philosophie. Erster Teil. Die Logik*, Vol. VIII of *Sämtliche Werke*, ed. H. Glockner (Stuttgart: Fr. Frommanns, 1929), Zusatz to § 82, 197. The English translation is from W. Wallace, *The Logic of Hegel* (2d ed. rev.; London: Oxford University Press, 1963), 153-154.
[2]   *Wissenschaft der Logik, Erster Teil*, 38; Struthers & Johnston, I, 67; Miller, 56.
[3]   *Wissenschaft der Logik, Zweiter Teil*, 59-60; Struthers & Johnston, II, 68; Miller, 440.

Hegel sees in ordinary words one important repository, hitherto unexamined, of the speculative truths present in common experience and language.

A. SPECULATIVE ELEMENTS IN ORDINARY LANGUAGE

Hegel's appeal to ordinary language as revelatory of deeper meaning takes many forms. The most arbitrary form is usually for purposes of edification; Hegel is merely interested in showing that everyday uses of certain words reflect certain significant aspects of a deeper non-immediate philosophical meaning.[4] Such maneuvers are unworthy of serious intellectual consideration, but they do reveal Hegel's intense desire to show that a deeper meaning is present in our natural, immediate expressions and experiences. More serious, however, are his constant references to and usage of puns and etymologies to make a philosophical point. All this is done with a view to revealing the essentially rational nature of human expression.

[4] For example, Hegel, points out that when we speak of a book without content, we don't mean that there is nothing there, i.e., that nothing was seen on the pages, but that "content" refers to something beyond the physical, perceived presence of printed words. Thus the common linguistic usage of ordinary consciousness points to a non-sensuous dimension.

"Nun aber bleiben auch schon das gewöhnliche Bewusstsein und der allgemeine Sprachgebrauch rücksichtlich dessen, was unter Inhalt verstanden wird, keineswegs bloss bei der sinnlichen Wahrnehmbarkeit noch überhaupt beim blossen Dasein stehen". *System der Philosophie, Erster Teil*, Zusatz zu § 133, 304; *The Logic of Hegel*, 244.

Hegel's attempt to appeal to ordinary usage and his desire to extrapolate speculative implications therefrom appear at times almost laughable. One of the best examples of this is his discussion of the ordinary meanings of the word "speculation" itself!

"Im gemeinen Leben pflegt der Ausdruck *Spekulation* in einem sehr vagen und zugleich untergeordneten Sinn gebraucht zu werden, so z. B. wenn von Heiraths-oder Handelspekulationen die Rede ist, worunter dann nur so viel verstanden wird, einerseits, dass über das unmittelbar Vorhandene hinausgegangen werden soll, und andererseits, dass dasjenige, was den Inhalt solcher Spekulationen bildet, zunächst nur ein Subjektives ist, jedoch nicht ein solches bleiben, sondern realisiert oder in Objektivität übersetzt werden soll". *System der Philosophie, Erster Teil*, Zusatz zu § 82, 196-197; *The Logic of Hegel*, 153.

Hegel explains the rationale behind his playing upon words and popular etymologizing in both the Preface to the Second Edition and the Introduction to the *Wissenschaft der Logik*.[5] He notes that logical categories, constituting the forms of human thinking itself, lie hidden in our familiar ways of speaking.[6] It is precisely the familiarity and unthinking immediacy of natural usage which enables us to pass over the speculative dimension of common words, thereby preventing us from realizing the deeper implications of our ordinary thoughts and expressions. Thus, referring to his statement in the Preface to the *Phänomenologie*, "What is familiar is not known simply because it is familiar",[7] Hegel asks,

what is more familiar than just those determinations of thought of which we make use at every turn, which proceed out of our mouths with every sentence that we speak?[8]

In attempting to lay bare the conceptual framework and basis of experience and thought, we must first bring to the fore the categories of what Hegel calls a "Natural Logic" whose presence in ordinary language has become submerged because of practical interests. Logic must concern itself therefore not with the coining of a new esoteric language, but rather with the reconstruction and deduction of such categories and thought-determinations *(Denkbestimmungen)* out of the content and form of ordinary language. Such *Denk-*

[5] Josiah Royce notes Hegel's use of such devices in his excellent article, "Hegel's Terminology", but does not attempt to relate it in any way to his broader philosophical concerns. Royce says, "Hegel was fond, like Plato and Aristotle, of etymological comments on the supposed origin and meaning of his terms; and in view of the state of the science of language at the time, his etymologies are often decidedly arbitrary. Deliberate plays upon words are also frequent". *Dictionary of Philosophy and Psychology*, ed. J. M. Baldwin (New York; Peter Smith, 1940), I, 445.

[6] Whatever man "zur Sprache macht und in ihr äussert, enthält eingehüllter [sic], vermischter [sic], oder herausgearbeitet, eine Kategorie; ..." *Wissenschaft der Logik, Erster Teil*, 10; Struthers & Johnston, I, 41; Miller, 32.

[7] "Das Bekannte überhaupt ist darum, weil es *bekannt* ist, nicht erkannt". *Phänomenologie*, 28; Kaufmann, Hegel, 406; Baillie, 92. Note the word-play here on *"bekannt"* and *"erkannt"*.

[8] *Wissenschaft der Logik, Erster Teil*, 11; Struthers & Johnston, I, 41; Miller, 33.

bestimmungen, Hegel says parenthetically, "run through our mind instinctively and unreflectively, and even though they enter into language, remain unidentified and unregarded".[9] Philosophy has to uncover the inherent logic – "the Logos, the reason of that which is, the Truth of what we call *a mere thing*"[10] – of our ordinary experience and language.

There is little need to list *ad nauseam* Hegel's plays on words and word-origins; they have been listed at some length in an extremely informative article by Alexandre Koyré.[11] Individually, such word-plays have no systematic significance and are usually sown throughout Hegel's writings whenever they conveniently fit in or make a striking impression. For the most part, Hegel does not draw any particular attention to his punning or etymologizing, except through hyphenation or italicization of the relevant words or syllables.

Hegel will, however, often inject a substantive comment when it concerns those words which, because of their possible contrary meanings or implications, illustrate the presence of the speculative in ordinary (German) language. For example,

many of its words have the... peculiarity that they have not only various, but even opposed, meanings, so that we must recognize here a speculative spirit in language; it is a joy to thought to stumble upon such words, and to meet with the union of opposites (a result of Speculative Thought which to Human Understanding seems senseless) in the naive shape of one word with opposite meanings registered in a dictionary.[12]

Two such words are worthy of our attention; the best known example is Hegel's use of *"Aufheben"*, which expresses "one of the most important concepts of philosophy". "To transcend *(aufheben)* has this double meaning, that it signifies to keep or to preserve and

9   *Wissenschaft der Logic, Erster Teil*, 19; Struthers & Johnston I, 48; Miller, 39.
10   *Wissenschaft der Logic*, 19; Struthers & Johnston I, 48; Miller, 39.
11   "Note sur la langue et la terminologie hégéliennes", *Revue Philosophique de la France et de l'Etranger*, CXII (1931), 406-439. Several more refined examples of Hegel's *"Etymologisierungen"* can be found in I. Fetscher, *Hegels Lehre vom Menschen:* Kommentar zu den §§ 387-482 der Enzyklopädie der Philosophischen Wissenschaften (Stuttgart: F. Frommann, 1970), 281, n. 279.
12   *Wissenschaft der Logik, Erster Teil*, 10; Struthers & Johnston, I, 40; Miller, 32.

also to make to cease, to finish".[13] The dictionary cites both the negative and positive meanings of *aufheben;* Hegel finds this use of one word for two opposing meanings striking and quite congenial to speculative thinking.[14] One should not bemoan the ambiguity or equivocality of such key philosophical terms; on the contrary, such words enable us to "recognize the speculative spirit in our language, rising above the mere 'either-or' of understanding".[15]

Hegel also makes an important dialectical point by playing on the various tenses of the verb "to be". Being *(Sein)* "is" and "is not", i.e., has been *(gewesen)*. Essence *(Wesen)* therefore is nothing but transcended Being *(Sein)*. The mediating and self-transcending process of knowledge therefore has a parallel etymologically as well as ontologically.[16]

B. THE SPECULATIVE PROPOSITION

Hegel's approach to ordinary language takes a more serious and systematic turn in his analysis of the propositional forms used to express certain types of judgments. He concentrates his examination upon various sentential forms of the "S is P" type in order to demonstrate the misleading quality of such propositions; in this connection, he discusses the limitations of a strict Aristotelian

[13] *Wissenschaft der Logik, Erster Teil*, 94; Struthers & Johnston, I, 119; Miller, 107.
[14] "Die angegebenen zwei Bestimmungen des *Aufhebens* können lexikalisch als zwei Bedeutungen dieses Wortes aufgeführt werden. Auffallend müsste es aber dabei sein, dass eine Sprache dazu gekommen ist, ein und dasselbe Wort für zwei entgegengesetzte Bestimmungen zu gebrauchen. Für das spekulative Denken ist es erfreulich, in der Sprache Wörter zu finden, welche eine spekulative Bedeutung an ihnen selbst haben: ..." *Wissenschaft der Logik*, I, 94; Struthers and Johnston, I, 119; Miller, 107.
[15] *System der Philosophie, Erster Teil*, Zusatz to §96, 229; *The Logic of Hegel*, 180.
[16] "Erst indem das Wissen sich aus dem unmittelbaren Sein *erinnert* durch diese Vermittlung findet es das Wesen. Die Sprache hat im Zeitwort *Sein* das Wesen in der vergangenen Zeit 'gewesen' behalten; denn das Wesen ist das vergangene, aber zeitlos vergangene Sein". *Wissenschaft der Logik, Zweiter Teil*, 3; Struthers & Johnston, II, 15; Miller, 389.

logic, based upon certain similarities among statements of identical grammatical construction. He attacks the basic laws of two-valued formal logic – i.e., the Laws of Identity, Excluded Middle and Contradiction – with a view to realizing his primary philosophical objective: the promotion of dialectical reasoning through an awareness of the limitations of the ordinary, static "either-or" judgments of understanding. In this section we shall analyze Hegel's notion of the Speculative Proposition *(Spekulative Satz)* with special attention to the specific role it plays in his philosophy and its implications for understanding the general relationship between philosophy and language in his thinking.

The ascription of qualities to a certain object or, grammatically, of predicates to a subject ("S is P"), seems to be a way of saying something about something *else*. Yet, if such statements or judgments (Hegel at times uses the words *"Satz"* and *"Urteil"* interchangeably) are to have any meaning and truth-value, "S" must have something in common – be "identical" in some way – with "P", otherwise such a statement cannot in any way be true, i.e., point out particular, actual relations persisting within the totality which can be conceptualized. If the relation between the subject and predicate of a proposition is completely identical, then we have an example of the *"Identical* judgment, and empty identical relation stating that the individual is the individual". If, on the other hand, the relation between the subject and predicate of a proposition is completely different (e.g., Hegel's example: "The Mind is no elephant".), then we have an example of the *"Infinite* judgment, in which we are presented with the total incompatibility of subject and object".[17] In modern parlance, the first is a tautology, while the second is an example of a "category mistake." In either case no meaningful particular truths are being stated.

The relationship between a subject and a predicate is not a strictly arbitrary, external one. The possibility of a meaningful proposition resulting depends upon an underlying "identity" be-

17   These two types of judgment are mentioned in § 173 of the *Enzyklopädie* (1830), 159; *The Logic of Hegel*, 306.

tween them. Use of the copula "is", which Hegel attacks as *geistlos*, leads us to think that we are combining or can combine two things which may have absolutely nothing in common with one another. But judgments *(Urteile)* are possible only because they reflect an underlying unity or "identity" of which the various poles ("S" and "P") are original parts *(Urteile)*.

Characteristically, Hegel, in introducing his discussion on Judgment, resorts to such punning to prepare the reader for his ideas and to justify his usage of the relevant terms. Thus the word "*Ur-teil*" is a better initial indicator of the ultimate meaning of *Urteil*, than any particular example of it!

The *etymological* meaning of the Judgment *(Urteil)* in German goes deeper, as it were declaring the unity of the notion to be primary, and its distinction to be the *original* partition. And that is what the Judgment really is.[18]

This underlying unity or identity is not a static one; statements about it cannot be *truly* understood and therefore are not really true, unless the relationship between reality and the categories ascribed to it is an on-going developing one. Furthermore, such a dynamic relationship must result from the self-differentiating and self-unifying activities of the knowing process of consciousness itself. According to Hegel's view, an understanding of his whole philosophy – expressed pithily in the words "Substance must be conceived and expressed as subject" – depends upon comprehending the nature of this process.

Only a study of the actual descriptions and states of consciousness and their dialectical development, as presented in the *Phänomenologie*, will really enable us to appreciate what Hegel means by the "Substance being Subject". We can get some idea of this notion, however, if we understand his conception of the *Spekulative Satz*, which he mentions often in his writings, but discusses in detail only in the Preface to the *Phänomenologie*.

[18] "Die *etymologische* Bedeutung des Urteils in unserer Sprache ist tiefer und drückt die Einheit des Begriffs als das Erste, und dessen Unterscheidung als die *ursprüngliche* Teilung aus, was das Urteil in Wahrheit ist". *Enzyklopädie* (1830), § 166, 155; *The Logic of Hegel*, 297.

Significantly, the best key for understanding Hegel's idea of *Spekulative Satz* and its essential relationship to his philosophy is in his play on the word "subject." By subject, Hegel first refers to that consciousness which slowly comes to realize that true knowledge of its object, its outside world, is really knowledge of itself and *vice versa*. Such a realization can only come about through the ongoing dialectical interaction of the subject-object relationship in which consciousness finds itself. It is precisely this progressive realization which forms the content of the *Phänomenologie des Geistes*. The self, or subject, sees itself and finds itself in another; it objectifies itself, or in Hegel's words, becomes "an other than it is for itself" as subject-consciousness. Finally, subject-consciousness "returns to itself" and the mediative process between self and its world – known now to exist in its own image – as well as the final result, constitutes ultimate truth. This is the meaning of Hegel's initial explanation of "substance being subject".

The living substance is, further, that being which is in truth subject or – to say the same thing in other words – which is in truth actual only insofar as it is the movement of positing itself, or the mediation between a self and its development into something different.[19]

However, Hegel also uses the word "subject" in its grammatical sense, as a part of speech: that which stands opposed to a predicate. His favorite "subject" is God, because it is precisely He whom most people use as *the* subject of any proposition which describes ultimate truth. God, as the true Absolute, is made the subject of numerous sentences, to which such predicates as eternal, love, moral, world order, etc., are appended. It should be clearly understood that Hegel does not deem it necessary to use "God" as a grammatical subject for his discussions concerning the Speculative proposition; its use is strictly exemplary. The speculative element can just as obviously be manifested in statements whose subjects refer to qualities or objects of a scientific or ethical nature.

Hegel's analysis therefore is operative upon any statements made by man which are meant to have a truth-value; such an intent is

---

[19]   *Phänomenologie*, 20; Kaufmann, 388; Baillie, 80.

obvious, since he introduces this analysis of *Spekulative Satz* by using the expression "all animals" rather than the word "God"; later, another example is "the actual is the general". The point he wishes to make, however, is the same: namely, that the most meaningful subject-objects are, initially, as grammatical subjects, merely general, empty names. They receive any true meaning or content they might have only through the predicates appended to them. Thus, for example, references to statements about God only gain their meaning by being mediated through various predicates which appear to be merely externally connected to their subject, but in fact are the basis of the subject (i.e., "God") having any meaning at all.

In saying that the subject gains recognition and identity only through its predicates, Hegel is demonstrating that the dialectical process present in reality itself is reflected and paralleled in the manner in which we make statements about that reality. To use the words "God is eternal", rather than "the Eternal", thus dispensing with the word "God" which has no meaning, but simply serves as a point of reference, is to recognize the dialectical connection between subject and predicate. Such propositions therefore embody the mediative process whereby the subject-consciousness gains knowledge.[20]

When such a statement as "God is Being" is really understood, one realizes that its weight or substance falls on the general predicate which alone grants meaning to the specific subject. We arrive at a paradox in that meaning and specification now reside in the predicate, which has given all content and character to the subject, the latter now seen as being merely a general term. In other words, the normal subject-predicate relationship is reversed

---

[20] "Das Bedürfnis, das Absolute als *Subjekt* vorzustellen, bediente sich der Sätze: *Gott* ist das Ewige, oder die moralische Weltordnung oder die Liebe usf. In solchen Sätzen ist das Wahre nur geradezu als Subjekt gesetzt, nicht aber als die Bewegung des sich in sich selbst Reflektierens dargestellt. Es wird in einem Satze der Art mit dem Worte: *Gott*, angefangen. Dies für sich ist ein sinnloser Laut, ein blosser Name; erst das Prädikat sagt, *was er ist*, ist seine Erfüllung und Bedeutung; der leere Anfang wird nur in diesem Ende ein wirkliches Wissen". *Phänomenologie*, 22; Baillie, 84.

and, in effect, the predicate is no longer the predicate, but the subject or substance itself.[21]

The connection between the *subject* as consciousness and the *subject* as a part of speech is clearly made by Hegel. The subject "moves" into the predicate and is in effect governed by it. This "movement" of the grammatical subject is possible only because it is really the movement of the knowing subject or ego. The motivating force, allowing the dialectical process between the subject and the predicate of a proposition to occur, is the conscious knowing subject. The subject of consciousness "replaces" the subject of grammar, and becomes the power which relates the various predicates one to the other in a meaningful organic fashion. Such a relation, however, is not arbitrary or purely subjective; the subject-consciousness has to conceptualize the object or event in a way that adequately reflects or conforms to its significance, its truth, and this depends upon it becoming aware of the underlying identity or unity, which governs the relation between a "subject" and its various predicates. The status of both "subjects" is determined therefore by the nature of their objects or what can be truly predicated of them.[22]

In becoming aware of the speculative nature of any statement, one must transcend the view that any static relationship exists between the subject and predicate of a sentence or the conscious

---

[21]   "In der weiteren Entwicklung des Urteils geschieht es dann, dass das Subjekt nicht bloss das unmittelbar Einzelne und das Prädikat nicht bloss das abstrakt Allgemeine bleibt; Subjekt und Prädikat erhalten demnächst auch die Bedeutung jenes, des Besonderen und des Allgemeinen und dieses, des Besonderen und des Einzelnen". *System der Philosophie, Erster Teil*, Zusatz to § 169, 369; *The Logic of Hegel*, 301.

[22]   Hegel's underlying play on the word "Subject" can be seen in the following citation, which also shows how the transition from one "subject" to another is effected.

"Sonst ist zuerst das Subjekt als das *gegenständliche* fixe Selbst zu Grunde gelegt; von hier aus geht die notwendige Bewegung zur Mannigfaltigkeit der Bestimmungen oder der Prädikate und das sie haltende Subjekt. Indem aber jenes erste Subjekt in die Bestimmungen selbst eingeht und ihre Seele ist, findet das zweite Subjekt, nämlich das wissende, jenes mit dem es schon fertig sein und worüber hinaus es in sich zurückgehen will, noch im Prädikate vor..." *Phänomenologie*, 50; Kaufmann, 444; Baillie, 119-120.

subject and its experience and knowledge of objects. In truth, a subject become a predicate and consciousness becomes self-consciousness by objectifying itself – becoming "an other than it is for itself". In effect, the "movement" of the grammatical subject in such a proposition microcosmically mirrors the process of knowledge of the subject-consciousness. Just as there is no passive, underlying subject that merely receives any and all predicates, so in learning consciousness does not remain unaffected, simply absorbing any experiences that come along. There is a certain order among the experiences of an initially "empty" or naive consciousness, witness the structure and development of the *Phänomenologie*, based upon the on-going change within consciousness itself. So there is a certain order to what can truly be predicated of an initially empty general name or subject. The speculative approach, therefore, breaks down any clear distinction of subject and predicate and reveals the underlying unity, the original identity, of which they are parts *(Ur-teile)*.[23]

C. THE SPECULATIVE ELEMENT IN THEOLOGICAL STATEMENTS

Though the speculative approach could conceivably be applied to any statements of a general "S is P" nature, Hegel utilizes it primarily to enable him to give an adequate explanation of theological truths and to justify the traditional religious language in which they are couched. The implicit speculative nature of language, implicit in most statements, becomes explicit only in the proposition of religious language because religion itself is that "stage of Spirit at which speculative content generally is the object of consciousness".[24] Statements and truths formally appearing to be contradictory or meaningless, and yet having religious and philosophic content, may reveal to us the speculative element present

---

[23] "die Natur des Urteils oder Satzes überhaupt, die den Unterschied des Subjekts und Prädikats in sich schliesst [wird zerstört] durch den spekulativen Satz..." *Phänomenologie*, 51; Kaufmann, 444; Baillie, 120.
[24] *Philosophie der Religion I*, 22; *Philosophy of Religion*, I, 40.

in language. Hegel makes particular use of the speculative approach, as outlined in the last section, in his analysis of the religious outlook and the statements made about its cognitive claims. The focal point for this discussion is the section on "Revealed Religion" in the *Phänomenologie*.

Hegel effects the transition from the highest form of art-religion (Comedy) to revealed religion (Christianity) through a speculative analysis of the statement "The Self is Absolute Being", the latter being the linguistic expression of the heightened subjectivity which characterizes the comic vein. The subject and predicate, respectively, of such a proposition "empty" or externalize themselves one into the other, thereby bringing about the dynamic distinction-within-unity which characterizes the speculative judgment or proposition. However, only through the cognitive process of the knowing consciousness do such propositions gain speculative significance. Therefore Hegel once more grounds the "movement" of the grammatical subject or predicate upon the intellectual operations of the knowing subject.

The concept has two aspects within it, which are represented as the two converse propositions above; one ["Being is the (Absolute) Self"] is that according to which *substance* externalizes itself from its state of substance and becomes self-consciousness, the other ["The Self is Absolute Being"] conversely, that *self-consciousness* objectifies itself and becomes 'thingness' or universal self-hood. Both encounter one another in this fashion, and therein originates their true union.[25]

Through such speculative treatment, Hegel seeks to dramatize the inadequacy of an either/or approach – the attitude of understanding – for dialectical, philosophical thinking. His final words in the *Phänomenologie* on this matter examine the problem of relying strictly on the laws of Identity and Contradiction when attempting to comprehend and express speculative truth. Ordinarily any judgment using the word "is" gives it a definite final meaning. "God is Nature" is therefore contradicted by the proposition "God is not Nature". Yet Hegel says, the truth is found in combining both these

---

[25] *Phänomenologie*, 525; Baillie, 755; Hyppolite, II, 263.

statements and realizing that both are necessary moments in the cognitive activity of consciousness, which ultimately is identified with the process of Spirit itself. The self-transcending nature of thought and its objects cannot be appreciated in the use of "is" or "is not" *per se;* they are mere copulas, spiritless, empty words. [26] The dialectical qualities of religious and philosophical thinking must retain the tension created by the juxtaposition of the "is" and the "is not". The difficulty which speculative thinking seeks to overcome is "due solely to sticking to the term 'is', and forgetting the character of thought, where the moments as much *are* as they are *not*, – are only the process which is Spirit". [27]

The realm of Spirit *as* Spirit is reached only when the laws of Identity and Contradiction are *aufgehoben.* This can best be seen in the meaningfulness of apparently contradictory statements about God or Absolute Spirit: contradiction itself is a manifestation of the Absolute. A statement gains speculative significance when its necessary relation to its opposite is made apparent and the transition from one to the other actually experienced. When contradictory statements find their "completion" in one another, the path towards the realm of Spirit is open. [28] Even in the most naive experience and expression of consciousness, as "Sense-Certainty", we witnessed how the "divine" speculative quality of language made consciousness express the opposite of what is meant. Precisely in contradicting itself, natural consciousness embarks on the road to Absolute knowledge and gains a glimmer of the experience it will undergo.

D. THE SCOPE OF RELIGIOUS THOUGHT AND LANGUAGE

Throughout most of his life, Hegel held a high opinion of the intellectual and theological content of Christianity. His feelings towards its more emotional and mystical aspects were, however,

[26]   *Phänomenologie,* 542-543; Baillie, 777.
[27]   *Phänomenologie,* 543; Baillie, 777.
[28]   *Phänomenologie,* 544; Baillie, 779.

ambivalent. He appreciated mystical writings only insofar as they pointed out the inadequacies of the usual categories of thought. As he said early in his life, concerning any communications with or about the Divine: "everything expressed about the Divine in the language of reflection is *eo ipso* contradictory".[29] The mystical is mysterious only for the formal "either-or" mentality of under-standing; otherwise, it is "synonymous with the speculative".[30] The necessity and rationale for mystical statements must however, be explicated, otherwise all we have is obscurantist *Schwärmerei*. Hegel could even rationalize the cultic aspects of religion as re-presenting in a concrete way, through man's identification with something objective, the reconciliation of subjectivity and objec-tivity.[31] Thus, the finite, formal categories of representational thinking are *aufgehoben* "in the faith in the One Spirit and in the devotion of worship".[32]

It is the intellectual content of religious thought and experience which primarily appealed to Hegel. He thought that the ultimate truths were the same for both Christianity and philosophy. Both deal with the relation between the finite and the infinite and both turn to God or Absolute Spirit to understand the true meaning of human existence.[33] Yet, although religious and philosophical con-

[29]   Knox, *On Christianity*, 256; *Hegels theologische Jugendschriften*, 306.
[30]   "das Mystische... (als gleichbedeutend mit dem Spekulativen)..." *System der Philosophie, Erster Teil*, Zusatz to § 82, p. 198; *The Logic of Hegel*, 154.
[31]   *System der Philosophie, Erster Teil*, Zusatz to §194, p. 404; *The Logic of Hegel*, 335.
[32]   *Enzyklopädie (1830)*, §565, p. 447; *Hegel's Philosophy of Mind*, 177. In the so-called "Systemfragment von 1800", Hegel discusses at length how, in the true worship of God, finitude and infinity, as well as subjectivity and objectivity, are transcended *(aufgehoben)*. Knox, *On Christianity*, 309-319; *Hegels theo-logische Jugendschriften*, 345-351.
[33]   Hegel stresses this theme often in his writings; the importance he attributed to it can be seen in the fact that it forms one of the main topics discussed in the opening paragraph to the *Enzyklopädie*. "[Philosophie] hat zwar ihre Gegen-stände zunächst mit der Religion gemeinschaftlich. Beide haben die *Wahrheit* zu ihrem Gegenstande und zwar im höchsten Sinne, – in dem, dass *Gott* die Wahrheit und er *allein* die Wahrheit ist. Beide handeln dann ferner von dem Gebiete des Endlichen, von der *Natur* und dem *menschlichen Geiste*, deren Beziehung aufeinander und auf Gott, als auf ihre Wahrheit". *Enzyklopädie* (1830), § 1, p. 33; *The Logic of Hegel*, 3.

sciousness are privy to the same truths, the quality of this awareness is not the same. Religion is an earlier stage than philosophy, but a necessary propaedeutic for it. Religious consciousness operates through the use of *Vorstellungen* in order to represent its truth. The intellect first visualizes in concrete images, before it can think or incorporate its ideas and notions into a purely abstract scheme.

To think and speak in religious terms has its limitations. *Vorstellungen* – mental images or ideas – are in effect meaningful symbols, which can represent the intellectual awareness and progress of consciousness in its proper perspective. But a true understanding of such *Vorstellungen* as "metaphors of thoughts and concepts"[34] of necessity presupposes philosophical training; otherwise their true meaning and interconnection is lost. An untutored religious soul is enamored with the emotional or historical dimensions of such symbols and the people who embody them. To associate ultimate social, ethical and, finally, metaphysical truths with such words (and the images they conjure up) as "Fall", "Creation", and "Incarnation" can be intellectually fruitful and worthwhile. But

the *Vorstellen* of the religious communion is not this conceptual thinking, but has the content without its necessity and brings into the realm of pure consciousness the natural relations of Father and Son instead of conceptual formulation.[35]

Such pictorial thinking and language do not divulge the inner logical necessity between one event or idea and another. Revelation initially comes from an alien source who is "out there" telling us what is true and how to act accordingly. True conceptualization and philosophic thinking can occur only when the dialectical inter-

---

[34]   *Enzyklopädie* (1830), §3, p. 36; *The Logic of Hegel*, 7. Hegel is aware of the emotional needs which such "metaphors" fill and realizes the dangers of metaphorical speech and imagery for strictly philosophical thinking.

"Die Metapher aber ist immer eine Unterbrechung des Vorstellungsganges und eine stete Zerstreuung, da sie Bilder erweckt und zueinanderstellt, welche nicht unmittelbar zur Sache und Bedeutung gehören und daher ebenso sehr auch von derselben fort zu Verwandtem und Fremdartigem herüberziehen". *Ästhetik I*, 539.

[35]   *Phänomenologie*, 535; Baillie, 767.

connections and development of man's experiences and thoughts are discovered. The language of the "Incarnation" or the "Trinity" reflect and represent the truths of Absolute knowledge without revealing the rationale for their order or existence.

The content and objectives of the two modes of knowledge are much the same, Hegel stresses, but the manner in which they are expressed is quite different. Religious expression is full of emotion-laden, pictorial images and therefore its appeal will always be more universal than that of scientific (i.e., speculative) thinking. Though the individual truths or objects referred to by the thinker and the theologian may be the same, they are, in Hegel's words, speaking two different languages. Only those who can think in speculative terms, and therefore have gone through or at least understand the peculiar nature of religious experience and knowledge, are equipped to evaluate critically the truths of various religions and philosophies.[36] Nevertheless, Hegel does think that for purposes of vivacity and convenience of communication, the allegorical clothing of theological terminology can often convey more quickly and simply the substance of purely abstract, conceptual thinking. The latter is the province only of the few who are willing to undergo the "exertion of conceptualizing" *("Anstrengung des Begriffs")*. Thus, for example, in explaining the nature of Logic as the system of pure reason and the realm of pure thought, he says,

---

[36] Hegel discusses this notion of the "two languages", non-speculative and speculative thinking, in the Preface to the second edition of the *Enzyklopädie*. The point he is making there is a critical one for our purposes. Its context is Hegel's polemic against those theologians who think that with sufficient dogma and piety, one can understand and criticize philosophy.

"*Der Gehalt* [of religion and philosophy] ist *derselbe*, aber wie Homer von einigen Dingen sagt, dass sie zwei Namen haben, den einen in der Sprache der Götter, den andern in der Sprache der übertägigen Menschen, so gibt es für jenen Gehalt zwei Sprachen, die eine des Gefühls, der Vorstellung und des verständigen, in endlichen Kategorien und einseitigen Abstraktionen nistenden Denkens, die andere des konkreten Begriffs. Wenn man von der Religion aus auch die Philosophie besprechen und beurteilen will, so ist mehr erforderlich, als nur die Gewohnheit der Sprache des übertägigen Bewusstseins zu haben". *Enzyklopädie (1830)*, 12; *The Logic of Hegel*, xx-xxi.

This realm is the Truth as it is, without in and for itself. One may therefore express it thus: that this content *shows forth God as he is in his eternal essence before the creation of Nature and of a Finite Spirit.*[37]

Late in his life, Hegel compliments one of his disciples, C. F. Göschel, in his review of the latter's book *Aphorismen über Nichtwissen und absolutes Wissen im Verhältnis zur christlichen Glaubenerkenntnis; Ein Beitrag zum Verständnis der Philosophie unserer Zeit,* for his ability "to work out the congruence of speculative thoughts with religious representations and to translate the words and signs of the one into the language of the other.[38] But although the language of religion and philosophy may correspond and each have absolute truth as its object, philosophic thinking alone can guarantee that the various *Vorstellungen* invoked by theological formulations are appropriate and do not pervert the speculative role for which they are intended.[39] Hegel invokes the familiar figure of speech of "two languages" to elaborate upon the relationship between the science of philosophy and the imaginative representation of religion.

Homer says of some heavenly bodies: they bear certain names among immortal gods, and other names among mortal man – so the language of *Vorstellung* differs from that of *Begriff.* Initially, man not only

---

[37]   *Wissenschaft der Logik, Erster Teil,* 31; Struthers & Johnston, I, 60; Miller, 50. In making the point that through grasping the inner meaning and conception of something, we gain knowledge of its true nature, Hegel says that this can be expressed in the language of religious representation.

"Der Begriff allein ist es, wodurch die Dinge in der Welt ihren Bestand haben, d.h. in der Sprache der religiösen Vorstellung, die Dinge sind das was sie sind nur durch den ihnen inwohnenden göttlichen und damit schöpferischen Gedanken". *System der Philosophie, Erster Teil,* Zusatz to §213, 425; *The Logic of Hegel,* 354.

[38]   In Göschel's book, Hegel is happy to find "die spekulativen Begriffe zur Anerkennung ihrer Übereinstimmung mit der religiösen Vorstellung herausgearbeitet und die Worte und Zeichen der einen in die Sprache der andern übersetzt...". *Berliner Schriften,* Vol. XI of *Sämtliche Werke,* ed. J. Hoffmeister (Hamburg: F. Meiner, 1956), 320.

[39]   As one writer has put it, "Pourrait-on comprendre que... Hegel reconnaît le langage religieux correspondant très exactement à son discours philosophique?... Pour Hegel, l'un et l'autre langage ont leur absolue vérité; il peut l'affirmer sans manquer de sincérité: c'est la tâche de la Philosophie spéculative d'en montrer le *comment*". Chapelle, A., *Hegel et la religion* (Paris: Éditions universitaires, 1964), I, 239.

recognizes matters mainly through the name of the *Vorstellung*, but through this name he, for the first time, becomes vividly familiar with it. Science must not only inscribe its ideas in the realms of abstraction (more abstract than those in which the immortal gods – not of truth, but of imagination dwell), but authenticate and specify their concrete embodiment. This, the immediate existential form which they receive in actual life, is the *Vorstellung*.[40]

Philosophy alone is able to authenticate and plot out which symbols, signs and words, will further man's intellectual progress. It is able to do so because the philosopher has traversed all other stages of experience and thought along with their respective kinds of linguistic expression. If philosophy is to have universal significance, it must create its own language through the use of other types of language and the *Vorstellungen* they invoke. Without incorporating the ordinary, non-speculative realm of communication and experience, speculative thought loses its claim of being able to represent to Spirit itself, i.e., the progressive comprehension and articulation of man's intellectual attainments and the rationale behind their ordered development. The perfection of a speculative language thus becomes a critical task for philosophy. In the final chapter Hegel's views on the requirements of a language *for* philosophy will be examined.

---

[40] *Berliner Schriften*, 318-319.

IX

PHILOSOPHY AND LANGUAGE

A. INEFFABILITY AND KNOWLEDGE

Throughout his writings, Hegel was preoccupied with dissolving any final dichotomy between form and content, between expression and what is expressed. We have seen the close relation between a certain level of consciousness and its mode of linguistic expression for Hegel. Furthermore, only when each level of experience of knowledge has been expressed, and statements about it examined, can that stage in the development of Spirit be systematically understood and resolved at a higher conceptual level. In the Preface to the *Phänomenologie*, Hegel bitterly attacked those who saw ultimate truth as immediately intuited, needing no recourse to any thought-out process of mediation and articulation. He also inveighed against the notion of ineffable truths – truths which cannot be expressed in language because of their utterly profound or immediate nature. When Hegel speaks of language, he refers to something capable of externalizing certain truths which can be articulated in a discursive, rational form. He attacked the idea that this cannot be expected in all cases; although it is the facts, and not the words that are crucial,

that does not give us permission to describe something in words not appropriate to it. For it is ineptitude and deception which claims that only the right *word* is lacking, and hides from itself the fact that it lacks the idea itself; if this were present, it would find the right word.[1]

Actually, the ineffable is only "something obscure, fermenting, which gains clarity only when it is capable of being put into words.

[1] *Phänomenologie*, 241; Baillie, 355.

Therefore words grant to thoughts their worthiest and truest form of existence".[2]

In this sense, Hegel's ideas run counter to the prevailing Romantic doctrine that finite human language is incapable *by its very nature*, and not merely accidentally or temporarily, of bridging the gap between human understanding and the infinite, divine Logos. Human language can never penetrate such a realm and therefore we must despair of ever adequately expressing the truths of absolute knowledge. Those who so attempt, soon realize that recourse to speech is a veil over, a check upon or a distortion of the living presence of the *Jenseits*, the beyond. God or ultimate reality lies, by definition, beyond all human discourse.[3]

Certain human experiences seem to lie beyond all manner of linguistic expression and explanation. But this is due to the present inadequacies of our expressive powers and not to the very nature of things. Hegel did not revel in such predicaments and did not employ them to illustrate the *true* nature of language or existence. Indeed, he often demonstrated (e.g., in the section on "Sense-

---

[2] *System der Philosophie, Dritter Teil*, Zusatz to §462, p. 355; *Hegel's Philosophy of Mind*, 221.

[3] Thus one author says that the *Stürmer und Dränger* saw "im Worte, in der Sprache ein Hemmnis, Verhüllung und Verbiegung des Schlechthin Lebendigen und Mächtigen... das Wort als menschlicher Ausdruck ist unzulängliches Symbol für das im göttlichen Logos Angeschaute und Erlebte..." K. Nadler, "Hamann und Hegel", *Logos*, XX, Heft 2 (1931), 273. One author believes that contemporary religious thought may revert to believing in such a notion. "Thus modern faith may well directly contradict Hegel on the ultimate issue; asserting, after all, a radical incommensurability between the Word of God and the word of man, it may begin with a radical "No!" to the modern world, said in behalf of the Word of God". E. Fackenheim, *The Religious Dimension in Hegel's Thought* (Bloomington, Ind.: Indiana University Press, 1967), 13.

T. M. Knox wrongly imputes this notion to Hegel when he speculates that "the thinking of the Infinite, on Hegel's programme, could be conducted only in the Infinite's own language, in which thought and its expression might be supposed to coincide, and not in any human tongue". A Review of G. M. G. Mure's *A Study of Hegel's Logic* in *Philosophy*, XXVI, 97 (1951), 180-183. A recent article in fact criticizes Hegel for systematically attempting to talk about God or the Absolute and views such an endeavor as futile. F. C. Copleston, "Hegel and the Rationalisation of Mysticism", *Talk of God* (Royal Institute of Philosophy, Vol. II; London: MacMillan, 1967), 118-132.

Certainty") that such views concerning the basic ineffable nature of ultimate reality, when examined closely, prove to be utterly inadequate. Therefore, the inability of our usually reliable powers of speech and expression to articulate certain facts is a virtue and not a fault or limitation, since it usually indicates a misapprehension of reality itself. If such "ineffable" matters do have any truth-value, they will find eventual expression possibly within another context than the present one. For Hegel anything that does not find its effect, its truth expressed elsewhere, beyond its own isolated existence, does not really exist. This is one meaning which can be given to Hegel's famous dictum about the real *(wirklich)* being rational and *vice versa:* what "works" or has an effect upon others *(es wirkt, Wirkung, Wirklichkeit)* can ultimately be expressed and conceptualized. To be sure, each form of expression or language is eventually seen somehow to be inadequate, just as various gradations of conscious experience are evoked and then transcended, but ultimately truth and the possibility of its adequate expression coalesce in the realm of absolute knowledge.

B. THE LIMITS OF LANGUAGE FOR PHILOSOPHY

Though Hegel had confidence in the ability of language to express adequately and completely our thoughts, he was not a literalist. He warns against making distinctions or believing in conditions only because they exist in language.[4] His whole analysis of the *"Spekulative Satz"* represents an attempt to undercut the traditional Aristotelian subject-predicate distinction. Language does have its speculative uses, revealing to us certain deeper or more developed truths than those immediately present, but linguistic or grammatic distinctions do not always reveal differences in fact. One can always beat about with words *(sich mit Worten herumschlagen)* without any true understanding. Furthermore, it is often impossible to distinguish consistently or systematically between

---

[4] Such a distinction "nur im Worte liegt". *Phänomenologie*, 99; Baillie, 119.

those words which, though homonymous (e.g., the copulative versus the existential form of "is"), have profound differences in meaning, and those "linguistic superfluities" which are synonymous and therefore conceptually redundant. However, Hegel is neither consistent nor systematic himself about his etymologizing or punning; they are employed by him if they illustrate a philosophical point he wishes to make.[5]

Hegel mentions several reasons why we cannot rely upon statements *per se* made by consciousness to describe its experiences as the basis for any systematic, philosophical pursuit of knowledge. First and most obviously, most of our ordinary words and expressions are associated with their relevant concepts or things simply by convention and chance association.[6] Even if it turns out that the origins of language are not conventional, much of actual speech is a product of various contingent elements. Hegel warns against attempting any precise systematization or rationalization of all human types of expression, linguistic or non-linguistic.

In respect of Mind and its works, just as in the case of Nature, we must guard against being so far misled by a well-meant endeavor after rational knowledge, as to try to exhibit the necessity of phenomena which are marked by a decided contingency, or, as the phrase is, to construe them *a priori*. Thus in language (although it be, as it were, the body of thought) Chance still unquestionably plays a decided part; and the same is true of the creations of law, or art, etc.[7]

Philosophy can distinguish the rational elements present in contingent forms of human expression, but this can be done only when the language of individual or "national" consciousness is seen in its proper societal and historical perspective.[8]

---

[5] A. Koyré notes that Hegel does not employ these devices with a view to discovering or pointing out any primitive, ultimate meaning from which our speculative deliberations must begin. "Note sur la langue et la terminologie hégéliennes", 427-428.

[6] "Der überwiegende Teil der Töne einer Sprache ist aber mit den Vorstellungen, die dadurch ausgedrückt werden auf eine dem Gehalte nach zufällige Weise verknüpft...". *Ästhetik I*, 408-409.

[7] *The Logic of Hegel*, 265; *System der Philosophie, Erster Teil*, Zusatz to §145, 328.

[8] "Die Voreiligkeit der Sprache, und das Vorwärts- und Auseinandertreiben

This latter point leads to the main reason for Hegel's rejection of any systematic attempt at philosophical thinking primarily through language: speech does not exist in a vacuum.[9] Its speculative implications can be appreciated only within the context of an actual experienced situation, whether it be the experience of an individual, a group, or a nation. It is for this reason that most of Hegel's comments on language, as well as his display of the many possible types of language, each specifically conforming to a certain level of consciousness, is most apparent in the *Phänomenologie*. It is here that he describes, as we have seen above in great detail, the relationship between an individual or a society and the language it uses. Furthermore, he often shows how a certain type of language develops in a concrete situation and its relationship to the preceding and succeeding types of language and the experiences they reflect.

The study of language therefore gains its importance only when it is seen in the context of the dynamic experience of the consciousness (whether individual or collective) uttering it.

Otherwise, the most sublime statements, e.g., about the Absolute, are only so much "senseless declamation". Only through lived experience, or, vicariously through our appreciation of it and its setting, can the deepest truths which are spoken have real meaning. Hegel uses a simile to make this point concerning the apparently identical statements made by individuals of different backgrounds or experience.

The absolute idea may in this respect be compared to the old man who utters the same creed as the child, but for whom it is pregnant with the significance of a life-time. Even if the child understands the truths of

---

der Nationen hat erst teils in Berührung mit Staaten, teils durch eigenen Beginn der Staatsbildung Bedeutung und Interesse für die concrete Vernunft gewonnen". *Vorlesungen über die Philosophie der Geschichte*, Vol. XI of *Sämtliche Werke*, ed., Glockner (Stuttgart: Fr. Frommanns, 1928), 100; *Lectures on the Philosophy of History*, trans. J. Sibree (New York: Dover, 1956), 63.

[9] In his review of Hamann's works, Hegel says that one cannot rely solely upon the character of language for a solution to central philosophical problems. "Hamann stellt sich in die Mitte des Problems der Vernunft und trägt die Auflösung desselben vor; er fasst diese aber in der Gestalt der *Sprache*". "Hamanns Schriften", *Berliner Schriften*, 270.

religion, he cannot but imagine them to be something outside of which lies the whole of life and the whole of the world.[10]

In Chapter III we saw how Jesus, and later John, were not understood by the Jews. Their experiences and their levels of consciousness differed and therefore the same objective words and phrases had totally different meanings and implications.[11]

C. THE LANGUAGE OF PHILOSOPHY

We can now begin to trace the elements necessary for the language of philosophy itself. As the culmination and logical development of all previous "languages" and their correlative stages of consciousness, the language of philosophy represents a fusion of the many qualities and modes of expression hitherto examined. The most important quality of the language of philosophy is its living, exoteric nature. *Man should philosophize in his own language and idiom.*

For purposes of strengthening the regular categories of Understanding, it may be initially necessary to learn a foreign, especially a classical, language. Such an endeavor enables one to achieve that distance (or alienation, as Hegel calls it) necessary for perfecting one's ordinary conceptual powers. Eventually, however, a person and a people must be able to articulate the true meaning of their experiences, their lived situations in their own language. They must be able to overcome that distance or alienation present to consciousness, through the vehicle of language. We have seen how often Hegel, in his early writings, stressed the necessity of a people developing its own language, grounded upon its own experiences, history and internal and external relations. Hegel continues to

---

[10] *The Logic of Hegel*, 375; *System der Philosophie, Erster Teil*, Zusatz to §237, p. 447.

[11] "diese immer objektive Sprache findet daher allein im Geiste des Lesers Sinn und Gewicht, und einen so verschiedenen, als verschieden die Beziehungen des Lebens und die Entgegensetzung des Lebendigen und des Toten zum Bewusstsein gekommen ist". *Hegels Theologische Jugendschriften*, 306; Knox, *On Christianity*, 256-257.

stress this importance of speaking and thinking in one's own language in his later writings, adding that such a condition (his favorite example being Luther's translation of the Bible into German) is necessary for an individual or a nation to attain freedom. Hegel explicitly identifies the actual possibility and historical beginning of freedom with the ability of a people to express its highest speculative aspirations, both religious and philosophical, in its own language.[12]

Hegel's emphasis on the need for speculative thinking in one's own language, and not in a foreign or formal one, leads him to making several important comments on the relationship between philosophy and its terminology. Most significant is his attempt to show how philosophy can appropriate ordinary language for its own purposes. Common words will not reflect or express ultimate conceptual categories and this should not be expected; after all, they are adapted to ordinary life, whose thinking is done through images or representations and not abstract ideas. It is the role of philosophy to recognize the speculative implications and connections, and hence justify the propriety of whatever *Vorstellungen* are used.[13] It can, for its own purposes, choose those words which approximate or hint at conceptual distinctions and categories.

[12] Thus Hegel says of a people: "hier bei sich selbst in seinem Eigentum zu sein, in seiner Sprache zu sprechen, zu denken, gehört ebenso zur Form der Befreiung. Dies ist von unendlicher Wichtigkeit. Luther hätte nicht seine Reformation vollendet, ohne die Bibel in's Deutsche zu übersetzen; und nicht ohne diese Form, in eigener Sprache zu denken, hätte die subjective Freiheit bestehen können". *Geschichte der Philosophie*, *III*, 257; *History of Philosophy*, III, 150.
[13] "Die Philosophie hat das Recht, aus der Sprache des gemeinen Lebens, welche für die Welt der Vorstellungen gemacht ist, solche Ausdrücke zu wählen, welche den Bestimmungen des Begriffs *nahe zu kommen scheinen*. Es kann nicht darum zu tun sein, für ein aus der Sprache des gemeinen Lebens gewähltes Wort zu *erweisen*, dass man auch im gemeinen Leben denselben Begriff damit verbinde, für welchen es die Philosophie gebraucht; denn das gemeine Leben hat keine Begriffe, sondern Vorstellungen, und es ist die Philosophie selbst, den Begriff dessen zu erkennen, was sonst blosse Vorstellung ist". *Wissenschaft der Logik, Zweiter Teil*, 357; Struthers & Johnston, II, 346-347; Miller, 708.
Many of the requisite speculative distinctions are already hinted at in common usage, though such words may be used synonymously. Thus Hegel continues,

It must therefore suffice if in these expressions which are used for philosophic determinations imagination has some vague idea of their distinction, as should be the case with those expressions, so that in them certain shades of the image are recognized which are more closely related to the corresponding Notion.[14]

The introduction of consciousness, individual or collective, into the realm of speculative thought and thereby into the possibility of its own intellectual development and freedom depend upon the nature of its own spoken language. In this respect, Hegel, like many of his contemporaries, saw in the linguistic development of a people a determining factor in their cultural progress. This reciprocal relationship between language and *Bildung* is a common theme of Hegel's. The backwardness of the Chinese people, for example, is due to the awkward hieroglyphic nature of their language. Indeed, anyone who has studied the comparative ways in which different languages express their ideas

is capable of discerning the spirit and the culture of a people in the grammar of their language. Those same dry Rules and Forms have now for him a full and living value. Through grammar he can recognize the expression of mind in general – that is, Logic.[15]

This last citation expresses more specifically the role of language in the intellectual and cultural development of human consciousness. Although Hegel strongly believed in the concrete exoteric nature of a natural language for expressing philosophical ideas, and therefore rejoiced in any speculative elements such a language might contain, he saw all languages as being potentially able to arrive at the articulation of the categories of logic. Therefore, although *individual* language are throughout conventional, their respective structures are anchored in the same universal activity of

---

"die Philosophie [wird] ohnehin die Freiheit haben, solchen leeren Überfluss der Sprache für ihre Unterschiede zu benutzen". *Wissenschaft der Logik, Zweiter Teil*, 358; Struthers & Johnston, II, 347; Miller, 709.

[14] Struthers and Johnston, II, 347; *Wissenschaft der Logik, Zweiter Teil*, 357; Miller, 709.

[15] Struthers & Johnston, I, 68; *Wissenschaft der Logik, Erster Teil*, 39; Miller, 57.

knowing, expressing consciousness. Hegel thought that further investigations into the origins of language – a developing area of study and speculation at that time – might reveal that the connection between a word-tone and the idea or object it signifies is not completely arbitrary, and that "the difference between one language and another consists in this that the same idea is expressed through a different sound".[16]

Although all languages may embody the same underlying logic, though at different stages of development, the need for relating and connecting ordinary thought and language with that of philosophy would be seriously undermined if we attempted to substitute a universal philosophical language, formal or otherwise, for the individual natural languages of consciousness.[17] To be sure, we can arrive at the general thought patterns of Understanding *(Verstand)* through the study of foreign, or preferably classical languages. Perhaps for these initial purposes, the study of the categories and propositions of traditional logic may suffice, though Hegel thought the study of classical languages was a better propaedeutic.[18] But for comprehending the higher, dynamic categories of Reason *(Vernunft)*, one must utilize one's own natural language.

With proper direction, one can turn the vagaries of ordinary language to philosophical benefit, as Hegel demonstrated with his use of the German language in his own writings. Though such punning and etymologizing are based on chance elements in the language, their speculative uses should not be neglected. In fact, it is because of this character of the German language and the level of culture and consciousness it reflects, that Hegel feels that "philosophy for the most part requires no peculiar terminology".[19] At the same time, however, since "some words from foreign languages (which indeed have already acquired by prescription the

[16]   Osmaston, II, 9; *Ästhetik*, I 409.
[17]   Hegel's objections to such a formal language were outlined in Chapter VII, Section C.
[18]   For example, Hegel's letter to his friend Niethammer, cited in Chapter I, note 9.
[19]   Struthers and Johnston I, 40; *Wissenschaft der Logik*, *Erster Teil*, 10; Miller, 32.

right of citizenship in the philosophic realm) have to be adopted in German... an affected purism would be least in place where it is the thing *(Sache)*... that is of capital importance".[20] Even when the requisite terms exist in one's own language, one may utilize Latin expressions, for example, for any necessary technical or artificial terminology because use of one's own language may result in an immediate unreflected understanding, whereas that of another will draw one's attention to the required mediated reflected nature of speculative knowledge.

Hegel's appreciation of his own language for speculative purposes is based, however, not merely upon such contingent etymologies and word-plays as *"Auf-heben"* and *"Ur-teil"*, which may happen to point to deeper truths, but also upon those elements of language peculiarly and specifically suited for expressing the categories of thinking, the *Denkbestimmungen*. These include not only various abstract nouns, but interestingly enough, prepositions and articles as well![21] Several uniquely Hegelian expressions are derived from the common usage of certain German prepositions or phrases; the best example of this is Hegel's use of *an (und für) sich* (commonly meaning in itself or *per se)* for denoting the primary methodological distinctions in his system.

---

[20] Struthers and Johnston I, 40; *Wissenschaft der Logik* I, 10; Miller, 32.

[21] "Es ist der Vorteil einer Sprache, wenn sie einen Reichtum an logischen Ausdrücken, nämlich eigentümlichen und abgesonderten, für die Denkbestimmungen selbst besitzt; von den Präpositionen, Artikeln, gehören schon viele solchen Verhältnissen an, die auf dem Denken beruhen". Hegel continues by comparing German to Chinese, where apparently such parts of speech are used more as prefixes or suffixes than as independent entities. He thinks it is "viel wichtiger... dass in einer Sprache die Denkbestimmungen zu Substantiven und Verben herausgestellt und so zur gegenständlichen Form gestempelt sind...". *Wissenschaft der Logik* I, 10; Struthers and Johnston, I, 40; Miller, 32.

Hegel even notes that at times the German language expresses certain conceptual distinctions which even Latin has not retained. For example, the important difference between being and "having been" (and therefore "not-being") – between Being *(Sein)* and Essence *(Wesen)* – which is preserved in the German language is not present in Latin, a language usually praised for its precisely reflected distinctions. In his words: "...das Ens begreift sowohl *Sein* als *Wesen* in sich, für welchen Unterschied unsere Sprache glücklicherweise den verschiedenen Ausdruck gerettet hat". *Wissenschaft der Logik, Erster Teil,* 46; Struthers & Johnston, I, 75; Miller, 63.

D. THE CONFLICT BETWEEN ORDINARY AND
SPECULATIVE LANGUAGE

If the language of philosophy is not to be a formal one, including many artificial terms and constructions, is it just made up of common words and sentences? What then distinguishes it from ordinary language? Given the rather narrow horizons of Hegel's analysis of the parts of speech (He talks mostly of words as names and only discusses propositions of the simple "S is P" form.), what is peculiarly distinctive of the speculative mode of expression in its systematic, philosophical form? Hegel makes several attempts at explicitly answering this question, yet he never comes to any explicit conclusions.

Hegel's most detailed examination of the inherent differences between speculative and non-speculative language is in the Preface to the *Phänomenologie*, immediately following his discussion of the notion of the *Spekulative Satz*. Such speculative propositions are superficially no different from other propositional forms. Therefore philosophy is reproached because, although its language does not seem distinctive and its propositions not unordinary, they cannot be as easily assimilated as other modes of expression and must be re-read several times.

Such a difficult endeavor, however, is what constitutes a necessary element of speculative thinking: the need to re-read the same propositions, each time to be sure on a more complex level. Only in this way is our common-sense view of such propositions and the distinctions they make changed. Initially, such determinations are viewed by ordinary consciousness as being either trivial or oracular; only gradually is this view destroyed and a genuine attempt made to understand such statements in a speculative context. Hegel describes the dialectical experience the reader himself must undergo, a procedure occasioned by the very difficulty and density of philosophical prose itself.

The philosophical proposition, being a proposition, gives rise to the opinion that the relation of subject and predicate and the procedure of knowledge are as usual. But the philosophical content destroys this procedure and this opinion; one learns that what one supposed was not what one was supposed to suppose; and this correction of one's opinion requires knowledge to return to the sentence and to reinterpret it.[22]

In effect, Hegel draws a parallel between the experience subject-consciousness undergoes *within* his system and the procedure that the reader *without* must follow to truly conceptualize it. Just as ordinary experience and language serve as the occasion for the beginning of philosophical wisdom (e.g., the situation of naive consciousness in "Sense-Certainty"), so the immediate, natural expressions of non-speculative thinking serve as the occasion for speculative thinking on the part of the reader. Yet philosophizing itself is possible only when what appear to be statements in ordinary language are, in fact, interpreted as breaking down the common patterns of thought.

The writer of philosophy, according to Hegel, must write in a natural language, initially preserving the associations and *Vorstellungen* of ordinary life and thought, yet at the same time add qualifications to such ordinary language which make the reader consciously aware of the need for transcending these common thought patterns. Such qualifications, serving as the foil to the ordinary non-speculative thinking which occasions all speculation, must be consciously expressed, thereby initiating the dialectical process of philosophizing. This procedure must be made explicit through the style and substance of the writing itself; if it is left to the imagination and intuition of the reader, and mere reference made to the need for such a procedure, then the necessary dialectical movement is usually lost on the reader.

Such a movement can be seen to be taking place in the speculative propositions themselves only when the actual subject who utters such propositions, or the philosophizing reader who wants to understand this process of consciousness, (Hegel distinguishes theoretically between these two situations by the terms *an-sich* and *für uns*, respectively) experiences the immediate natural situation, its consequent *Aufgehobensein*, and a final return to the same

---

[22] Kaufmann, 446; *Phänomenologie*, 52; Baillie, 122.

situation. Only such a dialectical movement, actually occurring through the conscious agency of the reader himself "is the actually speculative; and only the expression of this is speculative exposition".[23]

Throughout this section of the Preface to the *Phänomenologie*, Hegel grapples with the problem of using the particular elements and propositions of ordinary language, while at the same time exhibiting the manner in which the thought patterns of Understanding or mere abstract reasoning *(räsonnieren)* which such modes of exposition assume, can be transcended. On the one hand, Hegel hopes that it will be possible to avoid making the reader mix up these two superficially identical approaches (of speculative and non-speculative thinking) by perhaps avoiding the use of empty (proper) names which are usually taken to indicate purely passive underlying, unchanging subjects, as e.g., "God", and instead, employ more fluid conceptual terms such as "being or the One, the particular, the subject, etc."[24] Thus he thinks that while "the habit of construing the speculative predicate on the model of a proposition and not as Concept and essence constitutes an obstacle", it is one that could be "increased or diminished by the manner of the philosophic exposition".[25] Such an exposition, Hegel says, which "strictly precluded the usual relation of the parts of a sentence would attain the goal of being really vivid".[26] One could say that Hegel undertook just such a purely conceptual exposition in his *Wissenschaft der Logik*, where he analyzes "speculative predicates" as such (e.g., Being, Nothing, Becoming, Determinate Being [Dasein]) rather than treat them in the grammatical context in which they are found in ordinary language.[27] But even

[23]   Kaufmann, 448; *Phänomenologie*, 53; Baillie, 123.
[24]   Kaufmann, 448, 450; *Phänomenologie*, 54; Baillie, 124. Hegel's preference for such terms in discussions concerning the Absolute explains his positive attitude towards the mystical tradition in speculative thought, especially the medieval German one.
[25]   Kaufmann, 448; *Phänomenologie*, 54; Baillie, 124.
[26]   Kaufmann, 446; *Phänomenologie*, 52; Baillie, 122.
[27]   But any such systematic treatment of the role of language in Hegel's "Logic" would presuppose a different notion of language than the one con-

if such an exposition is possible, it would not be completely desirable or successful, for speculative thinking must, nevertheless, be anchored in, and often occasioned by, ordinary thought and language. Thus Hegel concludes that the tension between the two styles is a recurrent one and "therefore appears... to be a feature of the matter itself".[28] This necessary conflict, between the two modes of expression, that of ordinary thought and that of philosophical speculation, reflects itself in all of Hegel's writings subsequent to the *Phänomenologie*, and helps us to understand the reason why a thinker, so conscious of the need for writing philosophy in the medium of one's own ordinary natural language, has been characterized by many as the most esoteric and obscure stylist in the history of Western thought.

E. HEGEL AS PHILOSOPHICAL STYLIST

Much has been written about Hegel as a philosophical stylist; the comments concerning his manner of writing and his terminology usually take one of several forms. There are those – especially in the English-speaking world – who see Hegel's writing (and usually his thought) as a gigantic impenetrable smoke-screen, representing the epitome of obscurantist German metaphysics. Such thinkers (e.g., John Stuart Mill) saw Hegel's role in the history of thought as demonstrating the ridiculousness of absolute idealism, by reducing it to an absurdity, both philosophically and terminologically.

At the other end of the spectrum are those encomiums of German commentators on Hegel who see in his terminology as well as in his

---

sistently discussed by Hegel elsewhere in his writings. Such an undertaking is, unfortunately, beyond the scope of this work. Before one could undertake such a treatment, however, a full justification of interpreting language for Hegel in some non-ordinary sense would be needed. Such a *Hermeneutik* has been suggested by such thinkers as H.-G. Gadamer ("Die Idee der Hegelschen Logik", *Hegels Dialektik: Fünf hermeneutische Studien* [Tübingen: J. C. B. Mohr (Paul Siebeck), 1971] 49-69.), but thus far such attempts have contributed little to a systematic understanding of the "Logic" itself or the exact role of language in it.
[28]   Kaufmann, 446; *Phänomenologie*, 53; Baillie, 123.

philosophy, the culmination and integration of many "languages" in the German speculative tradition (e.g., Luther's language and the languages of the German mystical and pietistic traditions). Such writers stress many of Hegel's ideas on language and its usage, especially those elements characteristic of the German language which we have discussed in the previous chapter. They note, among other things, his use of ambivalent words and his appeals to ordinary language. Such attempts are very helpful to the non-native German reader, since they draw attention to aspects of Hegel's style which might otherwise escape him, but such comments seem very apologetic and attempt to justify almost every vagary of his style.[29] Comments are made concerning Hegel's "stretching to the limits the capabilities of linguistic expression"[30] and "the captivating originality of the plastic energy of his expression".[31] Comments are often made on how such modes of expression relate to his remarks on language, and the general attitude of his age towards the power of language, as exemplified in particular in the writings of Wilhelm von Humboldt. What such writers say may be partially true, but there is a strained air about it, and one gets the feeling that these writers are justifying him not only as Hegelians in the eyes of non-Hegelians, but as Germans in the eyes of non-Germans. One corollary of this general position is that Hegel's language cannot be translated if its speculative power is to be appreciated.[32] Such a view not only in effect turns Hegel into a poet or prose writer, but also denies the possibility of judging his work strictly on philosophical grounds – a result totally at odds with Hegel's *wissenschaftliche* endeavor.

[29]   An extreme example of this approach is found in Ernst Bloch, *Subjekt-Objekt: Erläuterungen zu Hegel* (Frankfurt a/M: Suhrkamp, 1971), 18-26.
[30]   H. Glockner, *Hegel*, Vol. I: *Die Voraussetzungen der Hegelschen Philosophie* (3d ed. rev.; Stuttgart: Fr. Frommanns, 1934), 42. A detailed and determined justification of Hegel's philosophical language is found in this book, 33-34.
[31]   Hönigswald, R., "Gedanken zur Philosophie Hegels", *Preussische Jahrbücher*, vol. 226, no. 2 (1931), 159.
[32]   "Auf keine Weise vermag durch diese fremdartigen Worthüllen die spekulative Kraft hindurchzuscheinen, die in den entsprechenden deutschen Worten und ihrem vielfältig ausgebreiteten Wortfelde mitklingt". Gadamer, *Hegels Dialektik*, 93.

Between the extremes of total rejection and uncritical adulation, it is possible to find a mean which does justice to Hegel's mode of expression, while at the same time realizing its limitations. It is known that Hegel could write in a charming, exoteric fashion when the occasion warranted it. His earlier writings, the rich illustrative materials in the Zusätze to the *Enzyklopädie*, his post-humously published lectures, and his reviews and occasional essays (e.g., "Wer denkt abstrakt?") point to his literary ability. Perhaps the most consistently well-written and comprehensible portions of Hegel's writings are the various prefaces and introductions which he penned to his works. It is just as obvious, however, that Hegel thought that the "meat" of a philosophical text should not be written in such a fashion. Hegel wanted philosophy "to speak German", but its German was not to be merely the ordinary one. Many writers, starting with Heinrich Heine, have speculated that Hegel's difficult terminology is the result of the view, then prevalent in the German-speaking philosophical world, that there had to be a complete distinction between a man's popular and his philosophical works, and that therefore, the latter had to be "written in a thoroughly forbidding style".[33] Walter Kaufmann states that this was the case with Kant and Fichte; he continues by noting that two of Hegel's intellectual mentors, Aristotle and Spinoza, have given no "quarter to the general reader [nor] shown the slightest concern for popularity".[34] Thus, the perverse notion had arisen in German philosophy, epitomized in the writings of Hegel, that, although one could write clearly and concisely, one must not do so. Kaufmann also cites Nietzsche's view that German sobriety dictated that one cover up the underlying *esprit* of one's personality and *Weltanschauung*.[35]

Such an explanation is inadequate when dealing with a thinker like Hegel to whom the relation between the language of philosophy and philosophy itself was paramount. In Kant, for example, there is little, if any, relation between how he wrote his philosophy and

33 Kaufmann, *Hegel*, 117.
34 Kaufmann, *Hegel*, 118.
35 Kaufmann, *Hegel*, 119.

what that philosophy was. As radical as his thought may be, Kant followed certain conventions and utilized scholastic or Leibniz-Wollfian terminology; when necessary he used traditional Latin terms in a new fashion.

Kaufmann dismisses Hegel's style as the product of the usual obeisance to a contemporary convention, simply adding that it was wrongheaded at that. Hegel, however, was much more preoccupied with the problem of language in general and philosophical terminology in particular than any of his predecessors. His concern with the relation between the demands of philosophy and the limits of (ordinary) language was an overriding one. The problem of philosophical style for Hegel is *a problem that arises from his own system of thought;* it is not simply the product of a perverse convention of day.[36] In the preceding section of this chapter, we have seen how Hegel notes that philosophical language by its very nature must be reread several times. The problem with such prose is not that it is a strictly formal one, as the languages of science or technical philosophy may be, but that it retains a disconcerting similarity to ordinary language, while in truth dealing with a different realm of experience and knowledge. This leads one to lose patience with it, as one does not ordinarily do with a scientific, formal language, because it appears to be nothing but poorly used common language. However, such is the purpose of speculative thought, and therefore also its language: it must lead consciousness, either within the system or through the reader of it, from the exoteric to the esoteric. For this reason it cannot initially abandon the images and ideas of ordinary language and can never completely do away with them. Ordinary language and the consequent conflict between it and speculative thinking is essential to the philosophical endeavor itself and can never be utterly transcended.

---

[36] E. Fackenheim takes the same position: "Hegel is a compact writer and – still more important – a thinker of incredible complexity, and he tortures language to make it say at once what must be said at once. One is almost tempted to say: he *must* torture language. For as one tries to say differently exactly what Hegel says, one often ends up either saying much less, or else reverting to his own words". *The Religious Dimension of in Hegel's Thought,* 6.

To retain the necessary connection with common parlance and ordinary thinking, Hegel must therefore manipulate ordinary language rather than manufacture a novel terminology. Few, if any, of Hegel's terms are strictly new, but almost all of them subject hitherto familiar terms to novel usages. In this way, the reader's ordinary thought-patterns are broken down and his view of reality becomes more fluid. To accomplish this, it is necessary at times not only to transcend the ordinary categories of Understanding in a systematic fashion, but also to show their relation to the higher level of Reason by disconcerting usages, endless qualifications and odd combinations of common parts of speech, familiar words and images. The difficulty of Hegel's prose originates from this endeavor. True conceptualization and dialectical thinking can be encouraged and actualized only through a mode of expression which avoids the "usual relation of the parts of speech of a sentence...".[37] The same ordinary terms are often used, but through various forms of manipulation, a new mode of thinking will be revealed.[38]

Undoubtedly, Hegel often went to extremes in his attempt at forging a new philosophical terminology, which by its very nature had to recognize and incorporate older speculative as well as non-speculative ideas and terms. Whether or not Hegel's attempt at a new, more fluid mode of expression in his native German, was successful or not is not an issue that can be categorically and

---

[37]   Kaufmann, 446; *Phänomenologie*, 52; Baillie, 122.
[38]   One of the few thinkers to mention this problem in a critical, yet sympathetic fashion, is Josiah Royce. He notes that "a familiar source of technical names is the deliberate employment of an already familiar term in a meaning which is not only specialized, but specialized through an emphasis laid upon tendencies or purposes latent in the popular usage". Yet Royce concedes that this common procedure is, in Hegel's case, "rendered decidedly more baffling than usual by the two fold fact: (1) that the terms whose sense is thus transformed are already old technical terms, of a past usage no longer vague, but, as Hegel himself holds, rather too abstractly sharp in definition; and (2) that the change from the traditional usage is frequently very considerable, and concerns some of the most original features of the Hegelian system". "Hegel's Terminology", 454. Royce, however, never demonstrates the *necessary* connection between popular and philosophical usage.

finally resolved. One's opinions on this matter depend to a large extent on one's philosophical prejudices and training as well as on one's feeling for the German language. What can be concluded, however, is this: given the nature of Hegel's views on the relation between speculative and non-speculative thought and expression, he could not have really written his philosophy in a different fashion. Therefore, it is a misguided hope, reflecting a false dichotomy of his own thinking, to imagine that Hegel could somehow have expresses the identical thoughts in much clearer prose. Hegel's philosophical terminology is grounded upon his conception of philosophizing and the validity of this conception alone can serve as the justification for the language he used to express it.

CONCLUSION

Many commentators on Hegel have discussed the close relationship between thought and language in his philosophy without, however, making any systematic attempt to examine his writings in order to understand the nature of this relationship and the light it might shed on the role of language in his philosophy in general. Furthermore, most of these commentators concentrate on Hegel's comments on language in the *Enzyklopädie* or the *Wissenschaft der Logik*, thereby neglecting the character of language as a spoken, natural medium developed and used in characteristically different ways at certain levels in his philosophy. For example, though mentioning many of the critical passages concerning language in the *Phänomenologie*, Henri Lauener, in his monograph *Die Sprache in der Philosophie Hegels mit besonderer Berücksichtigung der Ästhetik*[1] says,

> Die Sprache... als das wahre Dasein des Geistes geht am klarsten in ihrer eigentümlichen Bedeutung aus dem Text der von 'der Erfahrung geläuterten' Enzyklopädie hervor..."[2]

However, the unoriginality and inadequacy of Hegel's comments on language in the *Enzyklopädie* should now be apparent from our study of its role in Hegel's other writings, especially the *Phänomenologie*. In his Foreword to the new edition of *Hegel's Philosophy of Mind*, J. N. Findlay comments on the inadequacy of Hegel's treatment of language in that work:

---

[1] (Bern: P. Haupt, 1962).
[2] Lauener, *Die Sprache*, 34.

The role of language is sketched in a long paragraph (§459), which, considering the wisdom Hegel often attributes to ordinary language, is noteworthy mainly for its chattiness: one would have welcomed an account of the way words mediate our whole vision of the world, but we have to be content with the doctrine of a substitutionary identification which liberates us from the immediacies of the spatio-temporal environment.[3]

The danger of relying primarily upon the *Enzyklopädie* as a basis for understanding Hegel's conception of language is especially apparent in the first chapter of G. R. G. Mure's book, *A Study of Hegel's Logic*[4] entitled "Language and Hegel's Logic". Because Mure is preoccupied with Hegel's systematic and logical concerns as evidenced in the *Enzyklopädie* and does not consult the *Phänomenologie*, his posthumous "Lectures", or the *Propädeutik*, to say nothing of Hegel's Jena or pre-Jena writings, one does gain a clear idea of what Hegel is doing in the *Enzyklopädie*, but no justice is, or can be done to the role or nature of language in the various non-philosophical disciplines (e.g., culture, art, religion). Mure may be justified in such an approach in the above work, since it does concern itself with Hegel's logic, but unfortunately, it colors his general view of Hegel's conception of language, as discussed by him in his latest work; *The Philosophy of Hegel*.[5] This work is meant to present Hegel's general views on various topics. Mure constantly notes Hegel's view of language as "articulate speech expressing thought"[6] or criticizes his "narrow confinement of language to the expression of the universal"[7] without realizing – as we have seen in the *Phänomenologie* and Hegel's earlier writings – such a view has broad and various implications, and is not as narrow as Mure would have us think.

[3] *Hegel's Philosophy of Mind*, xvii. M. Clark, in his article, "Meaning and Language in Hegel's Philosophy" (*Revue Philosophique de Louvain*, 58 [1960], 557-578), also orients himself primarily towards the nature and role of language within the *Enzyklopädie* and *Wissenschaft der Logik*.
[4] (Oxford: Clarendon Press, 1959), 1-27.
[5] London: Oxford University Press, 1965.
[6] Mure, *The Philosophy*, 67, n. 2; also 162, n. 2.
[7] Mure, *The Philosophy*, 190, n. 1.

Jean Hyppolite does mention Hegel's defense of natural language as a medium of philosophic discourse, and (following a common theme present in most of the writings of Wahl, Koyré and Kojève on Hegel) staunchly defends the existential, dialogical nature of Hegel's thought and language.[8] None of these French writers, however, has tried to show the systematic application and possible limitations of the role of language for Hegel. We have seen how Hegel related his conception of language to its role within his philosophy. Hegel saw language as the best means whereby the intellectual content of the individual levels of conscious experience and their dialectical interrelationships could be expressed. One of the necessary conditions for appropriating the higher spiritual truths of art, religion or philosophy is the ability to express and therefore truly think these truths in one's own natural language. Echoing his earliest views, Hegel says

the feeling was produced that a nation cannot be deemed civilized if it cannot express all the treasures of science in its own language, if it cannot move freely in that language whatever the topic discussed. The intimacy which characterizes the possession of our own language is lacking in the knowledge which we possess in a foreign language only. Such a knowledge is separated from us by a barrier which prevents it from genuinely coming home to our minds.[9]

Another related condition is that consciousness itself undergoes the lived experience of successively encountering and overcoming the gap between its apprehension of the world *(für sich)* and that world as it actually is *(an sich)*. The initial means for doing so, according to Hegel, is linguistic expression.

Each type of conscious experience has its particular form of

---

[8] Hyppolite concludes, "Le langage naturel apparait donc comme le milieu propre du discours philosophique..." *Logique et Existence* (Paris: Presses Universitaires de France, 1961), 65; on the role of dialogue and communication see *Ibid.*, 23ff.

See also, J. Wahl, "Hegel et Heidegger", *La pensée de Hegel*, A. Marietti (Paris: Bordas, 1957), 185-195; A. Koyré, "Note sur la langue..."; A. Kojève, *Introduction à la lecture de Hegel* (Saint-Amand, France: Gallimard, 1962), esp. 126ff.

[9] Knox, *On Christianity*, 322.

linguistic expression; it is a mistake to ground speculative knowledge upon the expressive forms of a previous age. The language of philosophy, like philosophy itself, is an ever-renewing, ever-developing process. Appeals to entrenched linguistic custom (e.g., the etymologizing of ordinary words) may give us an added source of illumination, just as might an appeal to any dimension of habitual experience in our ordinary world, but such devices cannot serve as the basis for extended philosophical speculation. Hegel is not systematic about his play on words nor interested primarily in the original meaning of key philosophical words.[10]

This is one point where Hegel differs from Heidegger, one of the few other German philosophers who has taken the problem of philosophical language seriously. In discussing a specific philosophic matter, Heidegger usually begins by analyzing the original meaning of the relevant Greek or German words. In wanting to return to the original undisclosed meaning of a word as embodying *per se* the true speculative implications of the concept it denotes, Heidegger's approach is quite foreign to Hegel's. Though Heidegger's interpretation of Hegel is beyond our scope, since he does not specifically treat Hegel's conception of language, attempts have been made to compare their respective views on the role of language for philosophy, in the light of Heidegger's distinctive view of Hegel.[11] Heidegger's examination of certain aspects of Hegel's thought can be found in his articles "Hegels Begriff der Erfahrung",[12] "Hegel und die Griechen",[13] and his essay *Identität und Differenz.*[14] Heidegger applies some of his distinctive notions to Hegel's thought, viz., that of "ontological difference" and the revealing-concealing nature of Being (in this case identified with

[10]   Koyré makes this point: "Hegel n'a pas la superstition des 'origines' et, parmi les significations que peut prendre un terme, il ne recherche nullement le 'sense primitif'". "Note sur la langue...", 428.
[11]   For example in J. Wahl, "Hegel et Heidegger".
[12]   *Holzwege* (Frankfurt am Main: V. Klostermann, 1963), 105-192.
[13]   *Die Gegenwart der Griechen im neueren Denken.* Festschrift für Hans-Georg Gadamer zum 60. Geburtstag (Tübingen: J. C. B. Mohr [Paul Siebeck], 1960), 43-57.
[14]   (Pfullingen: G. Neske, 1957).

Hegel's Absolute), with a view to illuminating his own thought while at the same time liberating Hegel's from the confines of traditional *Hegelforschung*. Admitting his arbitrary use of Hegelian terminology, Heidegger says,

Arising out of its own appropriateness, the language of thinking nevertheless calls forth the thought of another thinking [Heidegger's] into the clarity of its own thinking, in order to liberate the other [Hegel's] into its own particular essence.[15]

A more ambitious attempt at actually developing a theory of language in Hegel's thought has been made by Josef Simon, who interprets the essence of language in Hegel's thought as the ground for the dissimulation of the Absolute.[16] The "problem of language" is the problem of understanding how the various appearances of the Absolute, experienced through language, are grounded in the dissimulative nature of speech itself.[17] Simon, influenced by Heidegger's notion of the revealing-concealing nature of the Absolute, is less interested in simply examining Hegel's specific views on language than in developing a theory concerning the role of what he calls "articulative consciousness" *(sprachliche Bewusstsein)* in the necessary dissimulation of any (linguistic) appearance of the Absolute. In distinguishing between appearances of the Absolute in and through language and the Absolute itself, Simon often appeals to Heidegger's notion of "ontological difference".[18]

---

[15] "Die aus ihrem Geschick gewachsene Sprache des Denkens ruft jedoch das Gedachte eines anderen Denkens in die Helle ihres Denkens, um das Andere in sein eigenes Wesen frei zu geben". *Holzwege*, 143.

[16] "Indem wir das Wesen der Sprache selbst als Grund der Verstellung des Absoluten bei Hegel deuten, deuten wir damit das Wesen der Sprache als das Phänomen, das die Hegelsche Philosophie im Grunde beschreibt, indem sie das Absolute als wesentlich erscheinendes und sich in der Erscheinung verstellendes Absolutes versteht". J. Simon, *Das Problem der Sprache bei Hegel* (Köln: Photostelle der Universität Köln, 1957), 6.

[17] "Es liegt im Wesen der Sprache, dass sie ihr Wesen hinter ihrer Erscheinung verstellt". J. Simon, *Das Problem*, 306.

[18] For example, "In der Hegelschen Deutung der Dichtung ist das Wesen der Sprache ein ständiges Durchlaufen und Entwerfen der Heideggerschen 'ontologischen Differenz'". J. Simon, *Das Problem*, 190. Another example of a treat-

Heidegger's own interpretation of Hegel, as well as those inspired by it, are ingenious, but tendentious. One cannot distinguish two ontological or existential levels in Hegel – the ontic and ontological in Heidegger's terms – without doing great violence to the most distinctive characteristic of Hegelian philosophy: viz., that the Absolute, whatever its final status, is nothing but the experience and expression of consciousness – individual and collective – and has no existence or meaning beyond them. The *leitmotif* of Hegel's thought is the desire to comprehend adequately and systematically the various forms of human expression, such as language, and their social and historical interrelationships. Hegel's criticism of the intuitive, Romantic view of the Absolute and his attempt to express the religious idea of Incarnation in strictly philosophical terms testify to his rejection of any un-expressed, "ontological" notion of the Absolute.[19]

The importance of seeing the role of language in its proper historical and social context is reinforced by Hegel's preference for the spoken word. It is here that he breaks decisively with the Enlightenment tradition from which he adopted many of his earliest ideas concerning the nature of language and its relation to philosophy. Spoken language for Hegel stresses the non-formal

---

ment of our topic influenced by Heidegger is found in a monograph by W. Marx, *Absolute Reflexion und Sprache* (Frankfurt a/M: Vittorio Klostermann, 1967). Marx bases his rather suggestive interpretation upon an existential analysis of Hegel's discussion of the *Spekulative Satz*, concluding that the task of language for Hegel is to express "the return of Being into Dasein". (*Ibid.*, 26.) Marx, however, does not get much beyond the *Vorrede* to the *Phänomenologie*, though he does recognize the important role of language in this work as a whole. *Ibid.*, 8.

[19] More specifically, consciousness for Hegel operates dialectically completely on one level and the knowledge it gains in the end, and which "we" philosophers who observe the process from without already possess, is not a knowledge of a different being, but truer or different knowledge of the same being present to natural consciousness. But if there is only one level of existence or being in Hegel, then Jean Wahl's talk, for example (echoing Heidegger's own words) of a dialogue or dialectic "entre l'ontigue et l'ontologique c'est-à-dire entre les étants particuliers et l'idée d'être" ("Hegel et Heidegger", 190) is totally misleading. Wahl himself later says that "le tort de Hegel, d'après Heidegger, c'est peut-être d'avoir nivelé les différences entre l'être et l'étant...". *Ibid.*, 195.

dynamic character of language while retaining that intellectual element necessary for an existential form *(Dasein)* of Spirit. Spoken language, more than any written, certainly any formal one, is best capable of rendering transparent the dialectical process of experience; it is self-transcending, leaving one aware of nothing but the actual process itself. Hegel's references to language or linguistic usage, in illuminating any particular dialectical pattern demonstrate his recognition of the peculiar contextual elements resident in each individual experience and form of cognition. In fact, as Simon says in a later article, when Hegel speaks of language, he has a concrete linguistic situation in mind.[20]

One contemporary writer has developed some traditional criticisms of Hegel – specifically, those of Ludwig Feuerbach – but with particular reference to Hegel's conception of language.[21] J. Derbolav claims that the very nature of Hegel's philosophy made it incapable of doing justice to the element of individuality which any adequate "Sprachphilosophie" must take into account.[22] Derbolav develops Feuerbach's criticisms against Hegel,[23] stressing the latter's neglect of the primary, concrete "dialogical" situation necessary for understanding the nature of language and the experiences in which it originates. We have seen, on the contrary, that Hegel was very much aware of the relation between the actual experiences consciousness undergoes and the character and role

---

[20] "Das impliziert, dass Hegel, wenn er von Sprache spricht, immer an einen bestimmten Sprachzustand denkt, wie er sich in einer Lebenspraxis entwickelt hat, und nicht an Sprache allgemein". "Die Kategorien im 'gewöhnlichen' und im 'spekulativen' Satz: Bemerkungen zu Hegels Wissenschaftsbegriff", *Wiener Jahrbuch für Philosophie*, III (1970), 29.

[21] J. Derbolav, "Hegel und die Sprache", *Sprache-Schlüssel zur Welt: Festschrift für Leo Wisgerber* (Düsseldorf: Pädagogischer Verlag Schwann, 1959), 56-86.

[22] "Hegel hat sich die Individualität der Sprache – und sie ist die Grundlage und Voraussetzung jener sprachforscherischen Bemühungen – philosophisch nicht zum Problem werden lassen". J. Derbolav, *Sprache-Schlüssel*, 73-74.

[23] In Appendix A, I have dealt at length with Feuerbach's criticisms of Hegel's thought, with particular attention to their respective conceptions of language. Since this involves an exegesis of Feuerbach's position and his notion of an ideal philosophical language, matters not directly relevant to our concerns, I have relegated this discussion to an Appendix.

of language in these experiences. Hegel's appreciation of the rich
and variegated role that language plays in art, religion and philosophy is also not fully appreciated by Derbolav.[24]

While each level of knowledge or experience has its own form
of expression, it is nevertheless true that philosophy, as the culmination of human intellectual development, and concomitantly
philosophical language, are more adequate means for understanding
the nature of existence. Hegel does hold forth the possibility of a
natural language that will do justice to the modes of expression
which preceded it, both historically and logically, yet express more
than any one of them could individually. J. N. Findlay views
Hegel's systematic thinking (particularly his *Wissenschaft der
Logik*) as a series of linguistic recommendations, none of which
has ultimate truth or validity.[25] But if there is any sort of identity
between thought and language, as Findlay himself and many
others have claimed, then such a statement implies that no system
of philosophy is adequate. While the dialectical progression must
take its inevitable toll, nevertheless each "higher" or "later" form
of thinking and expression is truer and more valid than the one
preceding it.[26] The speculative language of philosophy does have

[24] As with most commentators on Hegel's conception of language, Derbolav's
remarks are inspired primarily by the ancillary role of language in the *Enzyklopädie*. For example: "Hegel hat die Sprache nur als Tat der theoretischen
Intelligenz begriffen und sich damit ihren praktischen Horizont verdunkelt;
er hat sie zu sehr auf die wissenschaftliche Aussageform festgelegt und ist darum
ihren übrigen Weisen der Sinnoffenbarung nicht gerecht geworden; die dich-
terische blieb in den vorsprachlichen Raum der Phantasie zurückverwiesen,
die moralische und religiöse mussten erst kunstvoll in theoretischen Sinn übersetzt werden". J. Derbolav, Sprache-Schlüssel, 78.
[25] "Hegel recommends for our adoption a given way of talking about the
world, then discovers flaws and inadequacies in this mode of speaking, then
supersedes it by a further recommendation which also comprehends it, until
his last recommendation supersedes and comprehends all others. It is obvious
that there can be no question (in the ordinary sense of the words) of either
truth or validity in such a series of recommendations. There can only be
questions regarding the linguistic or conceptual adequacy or satisfactoriness
of its terms". *Hegel: A Re-examination*, 151.
[26] W. H. Walsh justifies the existence, even if only regulative, of an ideal
speculative language and a final truth in Hegel as a necessary motive for any
dialectical thinking. The self-criticism of the dialectical process "would be

greater truth and does more adequately mirror the full intellectual expression of Spirit than previous modes of expression.

Furthermore, as we have seen in our analysis of the speculative proposition, only through the writing and reading of philosophy itself can one self-consciously recognize the conceptual exertion *(Anstrengung des Begriffs)* necessary to the attainment of philosophical truth. The language of philosophy which Hegel aims for would have a higher validity, not only logically or historically in the sense of a further or more developed and universal statement concerning the dialectical character of reality, but personally for the reader trying to live as well as think philosophically.

Can one say that Hegel had a philosophy of language? Throughout his writings, Hegel attempted to justify major dialectical moves in his thought, through an analysis of the ordinary language used to describe a particular experience or stage of consciousness. Although many thinkers – apart from the Romantic enthusiasts – saw language or Logos as an essential factor in understanding man's intellectual development,[27] Hegel is the first philosopher to attempt to understand the phenomenon of language within a broader and more organized framework and, ultimately, to see the danger for philosophy of interpreting everything through the medium of the spoken or written word.[28]

Already in the *Phänomenologie des Geistes*, language is no longer presented, as it was in his earlier *Jenenser Realphilosophie*, as a

---

impossible unless the critic had got beyond the stage of simply operating with a language: the thought of something better must also be present to his mind. And this something better, ...was the same in every case: a single ideal of adequate speech dominated all our linguistic operations, though it might be admitted that our awareness of it varied greatly from one level to another". "On the Philosophy of Hegel", *Philosophy*, XXVII (1953), 201.

[27] Herder, Rousseau, Hamann and Hegel's contemporary, Wilhelm von Humboldt, all discussed at length the intellectual and spiritual importance of language. See Koyré, "Note sur la langue...", 415.

[28] See Chapter IX, note 9.

specific stage in man's intellectual development, but rather becomes the medium for expressing the dialectical process of experience in general. Many of Hegel's earlier ideas about and insights into the nature of language are utilized for explaining and justifying the dialectical nature of experience itself. Language becomes too basic a category to be relegated to one stage of Spirit; in this sense, one can say that Hegel had a theory concerning language, much as he had one of dialectic, and that his theory of dialectic originated in part from his initial systematic attempts at a theory of signification and language.

It would be wrong, however, to say that Hegel had a developed philosophy of language. Other than his early attempts at a system, he never systematically presents his ideas on language, or brings them all together at a certain level of development of consciousness, the way he does with the disciplines of art, religion or philosophy (i.e., logic). Although language cuts across all these areas, history does much the same for Hegel, yet several of his major works do treat history in itself as well as expound the systematic relation of history to other areas of man's intellectual development. Language, however, for Hegel cannot be treated "in and for itself", and only if it were so treated as a separate discipline could one speak of "Hegel's Philosophy of Language". In this essay, we have tried to show why language is not, and could not be, a specific object of his thought, and why, nevertheless, a study of the role of language *within* Hegel's philosophy and his views on the use of language in writing philosophy illuminate critical aspects of his thought.

APPENDIX

FEUERBACH'S ATTACK ON HEGEL

In examining the role of language in Hegel's thought, Ludwig
Feuerbach's famous attack on Hegel, especially as it is presented
in his "Zur Kritik der Hegelschen Philosophie", should be mentioned.[1] Feuerbach uses the section on "Sense-Certainty" in the
Phänomenologie des Geistes as the basis for his criticism of Hegel's
refusal, or inability, to treat the individual objects and egos themselves in his system. Since then, the section on "Sense-Certainty"
has served as the *locus classicus* for those attacking Hegel's epistemology as "pan-logistic" and incapable of dealing with the individual as individual. Among such critics are Jacob Loewenberg
and Josef Derbolav, whose comments have been examined in the
body of this essay.

Feuerbach concentrates his attack upon Hegel's manipulation
of language in order to justify the existence of universals. Hegel's
argument is unconvincing precisely for those who hold to the
reality of sensuous being and think that the categories of thought
and language are bloodless and removed from reality.[2] To such a
consciousness, all words are proper names, mere signs; they are
unreal and empty. Language is not material to the argument, and
if any contradictions arise from it, then so much the worse for

---

[1]   This essay is found in *Philosophische Kritiken und Grundsätze*, ed. F. Jodl,
Vol. II of his *Sämtliche Werke*, ed. W. Bolin & F. Jodl (Stuttgart: Fr. Frommanns Verlag [E. Hauff], 1904), 158-204. Certain passages of his "Gründsätze
der Philosophie der Zukunft" are also relevant. *Ibid.*, 245-320.
[2]   In Feuerbach's pungent phrasing: "Die Sprache gehört hier gar *nicht zur
Sache*. Die Realität des sinnlichen einzelnen Seins ist uns eine mit unserem
Blute besiegelte Wahrheit". *Sämtliche Werke* II, 185.

language. Words don't replace things: to play with one proves nothing concerning the other.[3]

According to Feuerbach, Hegel does not discuss the actual physical "Here" or "Now", but only a logical and abstract form of it. He pretends to begin his investigation with that which is other than thought, yet thinks that such an "other" can be nevertheless comprehended by thought.[4] Language identifies Being with essence, thus robbing it of its sensuous heartfelt existence; such "thought out", spoken Being is artificial and unreal ("ein gemachtes, erdachtes Sein, ein Sein *ohne das Wesen* des Seins...").[5] Feuerbach wanted to replace the usual categories of thought with other patterns that would be ineffable, but have their own kind of meaning and rationality:

Being, based clearly upon such "inexpressibles" [as the real, non-logical objects] is itself something therefore ineffable – indeed the ineffable. Where words cease, life first begins, first discloses the secret of Being. If, for that reason, ineffability is irrationality, so is all existence irrational, because it is always only *this* existence. But this is not so; existence has – on its own account, even without being spoken – meaning and reason.[6]

Feuerbach's defense of the ineffability of actual being has that opaqueness and hint of deeper things that Hegel distrusts so much in his Preface to the *Phänomenologie*. Feuerbach did think that there was an original form of thought (and possibly language?) which we have not yet attained, and which is not merely a refraction of the primal forms. He discusses this position briefly in an interesting note, prefacing it with one of his usual unphilosophical arguments against language.

---

[3]   Feuerbach is quick to use ridicule instead of reasoning; such an approach makes for exciting reading, but at times, little else. Concerning words and things, for example, he says we can never live on spoken or logical bread, or as he lovingly calls it, *dem Brote an sich* – but only on this individual ineffable bread. *Sämtliche Werke* II, 288. Previously he claims that if we could not individuate things, it would lead to laughable legal problems; there would be only a community of wives and property, since there is no real difference between this and that, only universals.

[4]   *Sämtliche Werke* II, 187.

[5]   *Sämtliche Werke* II, 286.

[6]   *Sämtliche Werke* II, 288.

The so-called logical forms are only *abstract, rudimentary forms of speech*, but speaking is not thinking, otherwise the greatest babbler would be the greatest thinker. Our customary, so-called thinking is only the translation of a more or less obscurely known, difficulty understood, alien author, ingeniously operating upon us, into forms of language understood by us; only in this *translation*, and not in the original, are the so-called logical forms valid; they thereby pertain not to Optics, but to the *Dioptrics* of the Spirit – by all means, an unknown field as yet.[7]

Feuerbach's attack on Hegel's method in the first section of the *Phänomenologie* might appear justified. First of all, by emphasizing or abstracting one pole or another of the subject-object relation, Hegel would seem to be destroying that very immediacy which characterizes such sense experiences. Secondly, Hegel seems at times to be arguing about the statements that natural consciousness makes about its experience, rather than the experiences themselves. Such experiments as writing down statements of one's experience or playing the description of one state of consciousness off against another leave one with the impression that Hegel is not concerned with the concrete experience itself, but rather with certain abstract or mediated forms of it. One must turn to the objects themselves – get down to the facts – and forget about such word-games: "show me, *point out* to me what you are talking about", Feuerbach asks impatiently.[8] Feuerbach agrees with Hegel that the individual "thises" of sense-experience do disappear, but they are always replaced by *another* "this" and not by some over-arching, mysteriously injected universal. All we experience are these particulars of sense experience – not any sort of universal.[9]

Yet Hegel in effect has an answer to Feuerbach's criticism, by showing that pointing to the sense particulars, as in the third argument of "Sense-Certainty", merely *reinforces* the meaning of the words used to describe them, rather than undermining or counteracting them. Even when the immediate, ineffable subject-object relation is preserved, the result, as we have seen above, is

[7] *Sämtliche Werke* II, 172, note.
[8] *Sämtliche Werke* II, 185.
[9] *Sämtliche Werke* II, 186.

APPENDIX

the same. There is no such thing as a meaningful experience of a particular, apart from its relations with other particulars.

It is interesting to note that Feuerbach's own thoughts on language were much less sophisticated than Hegel's. Feuerbach viewed language primarily as a vehicle for articulating ready-made thoughts. Most of the time, however, the thoughts involved, and certainly the language, were a distortion of the true message one can gain from concrete sensuous existence. His attack on Hegel as described here is a good example of this tendency. Feuerbach's depreciation of language is heightened by his thoroughgoing nominalism: words are only proper names or signs, not relating themselves in any meaningful universal fashion to the things they signify, but being merely conventions. Hegel also adhered to a conventional theory of signs, but did think that the system that grew out of them and the manner in which it was employed involved something deeper. Language expresses the dialectical process inherent in the nature of the knowing activity of consciousness itself. Furthermore, Hegel did distinguish between demonstratives and proper nouns, thinking that both – in the proper denotative context – were merely arbitrary indicators or pointers. Yet Hegel felt that the usage of universals (such as demonstrative pronouns) as specific indicators pointed to an insight that was worth pursuing philosophically. The view that such pointers are nothing but proper nouns does not tell the whole story for him.[10]

Feuerbach did grant one role to language that has been adopted

[10] "The word 'this' serves to fix the distinction and that Something which is to be taken affirmatively. But 'this' clearly expresses that this distinction and emphasizing of one Something is a process of designation, subjective and external to the Something. The entire determinateness falls within this external designation, and even the expression 'this' contains no distinction; each and every Something is 'this' as much as it is also Other. We fancy that by 'this' we are expressing something perfectly definite, overlooking that language, being a work of understanding, expresses universals only, except when it *names* individual objects; the individual name, however, is meaningless in this sense that it expresses no universal, for which reason it also appears as something merely posited and arbitrary; and indeed proper names may be assumed, bestowed and also altered at will". Struthers & Johnston, I, 130; *Wissenschaft der Logic, Erster Teil*, 104-105; Miller, 117.

by later critics of Hegel: its function as the means for true inter-personal communication or dialogue.[11] If our thoughts are already well-formed and meaningful before we articulate them, as Feuerbach claims, then what is the purpose of language (as well as writing and demonstration)? Only to communicate these thoughts to others. Language's only function for Feuerbach is as a means for communicating thoughts and not articulating them; this is not so with Hegel. The spiritual and universal implications of language are found only in its role as a means of fostering communication and, ultimately, community, among individuals, and not as a critical element in the intellectual and spiritual development of the individual as such.

Language is nothing other than the *realization of the species*, the media-tion of the I with the Thou, in order to exhibit, through the transcending of their individual isolation, the unity of the species. The element of the word is thereby the air, the most spiritual and universal medium of Life.[12]

Language is thus seen by Feuerbach only as an external medium of communication, albeit a very important one. It is too categorical and universal-oriented to serve any meaningful role in the develop-ment of the individual as such.

Though Hegel thought that language did play an important role helping to create and also reflect that unity or community of individuals (viz., his discussions of the relation of language to *Volksgeist*), he saw as equally important, the role of language as a vehicle for expressing the dialectical process of the experience of the individual knower himself. Hegel's treatment of language is broader than Feuerbach's because Hegel realizes the important role that such a medium plays in the development of individual consciousness as well.

---

[11]   Buber's notion of "I-Thou" is directly traceable to Feuerbach's influence; see also Derbolav, 77ff.
[12]   Feuerbach, *Sämtliche Werke* II, 169-170.

SELECTED BIBLIOGRAPHY

I. WRITINGS BY HEGEL

A. Collected Works

Glockner, Hermann (ed.), *Sämtliche Werke: Jubiläumausgabe in 20 Bänden* (Stuttgart: Frommanns, 1927-30).
Supplements to *Jubiläumausgabe:*
Glockner, Hermann (ed.), *Hegel-Lexicon*, 2 vols. 2nd. ed. rev. (Stuttgart: Frommanns, 1957).
Hoffmeister, J. (ed.), *Dokumente zu Hegels Entwicklung* (Stuttgart: Frommanns, 1936).
Hoffmeister, J., Lasson, G., et al. *Sämtliche Werke: Kritische Ausgabe* (Leipzig and Hamburg: F. Meiner, 19—). This series is incomplete, with various volumes re-edited. Works consulted from this series are therefore cited individually below.
Hoffmeister, J. (ed.), *(Berliner Schriften*. Hamburg: F. Meiner, 1956).
Hoffmeister, J. and Flechsig, R. (eds.), *Briefe von und an Hegel*, 4 vols. (Hamburg: F. Meiner, 1952-1960).
Hoffmeister, J. (ed.), *Jenenser Realphilosophie, I: Die Vorlesungen von 1803/04, aus dem Manuskript* (Leipzig: F. Meiner, 1932).
—, *Jenenser Realphilosophie, II: Die Vorlesungen von 1805/06, aus dem Manuskript* (Leipzig: F. Meiner, 1931).
—, *Jenaer Realphilosophie. Vorlesungenmanuskripte zur Philosophie der Natur und des Geistes von 1805-1806* (Hamburg: F. Meiner, 1967) (Unrevised reissue of *Jenenser Realphilosophie*, II.)
—, *Nürnberger Schriften: Texte, Reden, Berichte und Gutachten zum Nürnberger Gymnasialunterricht: 1806-1816* (Leipzig: F. Meiner, 1938).
—, *Phänomenologie des Geistes.* (Hamburg: F. Meiner, 1952).
Lasson, G. (ed.). *Erste Druckschriften.* (Leipzig: F. Meiner, 1928).
—, *Schriften zur Politik und Richtsphilosophie.* (Leipzig: F. Meiner, 1913).
—, *Wissenschaft der Logik.* 2 vols. (Hamburg: F. Meiner, 1967).

B. Individual Works

Nicolin, F. and Pöggeler, O. (eds.), *Enzyklopädie der philosophischen Wissenschaften im Grundrisse (1830)* (Hamburg: F. Meiner, 1959).

Nohl, Herman (ed.), *Hegels theologische Jugendschriften, nach den Hand-schriften der Kgl. Bibliothek in Berlin* (Tübingen: Mohr [Paul Siebeck], 1907).

C. English and French Translations of Works

Baillie, J. B. (tr.), *The Phenomenology of Mind*. 2nd rev. ed. (London: George Allen & Unwin, 1955).

Carrère, Jean (tr.), *Hegel: Correspondance*, 3 vols. (Nayenne: Gallimard, 1962-71).

de Gaudillac, M. (tr.), *Propedeutique philosophique* (Paris: Éditions de Minuit, 1963).

Friedrich, Carl J. (ed.), *The Philosophy of Hegel* (New York: Modern Library, 1954).

Haldane, Elizabeth S. and Simson, F., *Lectures on the History of Philosophy*, 3 vols. (London: Kegan, Paul Trench, Trübner, & Co. 1892-96).

Hyppolite, J. (tr.), *La phénoménologie de l'esprit*, 2 vols. (Paris: Aubier, 1947).

Johnston, W. H. and Struthers, L. G. (trs.), *Science of Logic*, 2 vols. (London: Allen & Unwin, 1929).

Knox, T. M. (tr.), *Philosophy of Right* (Oxford: Clarendon Press, 1942).

Knox, T. M. (tr.), with an Introduction and Fragments Translated by Richard Kroner, *On Christianity: Early Theological Writings by Friedrich Hegel* (New York: Harper Torchbooks, 1961).

Miller, A. V. (tr.), With Foreword by J. N. Findlay, *Hegel's Philosophy of Nature* (Oxford: Clarendon Press, 1970).

Osmaston, F. P. B., *The Philosophy of Fine Art*, 4 vols. (London: G. Bell & Sons, 1920).

Sibree, J. (tr.), with an introduction by C. J. Friedrich, *Lectures on the Philosophy of History* (New York: Dover, 1956).

Speirs, E. B. and Sanderson, J. Burdon, *Lectures on the Philosophy of Religion, Together with a work on the Proof of the existence of God*, 3 vols. (London: Kegan Paul, Trench, Trübner, & Co., 1895).

Wallace, W. (tr.), with the *Zusätze* in Boumann's Text Translated by A. V. Miller, *Hegel's Philosophy of Mind* (Oxford: Clarendon Press, 1971).

—, (tr.), *The Logic of Hegel*, 2nd ed. rev. (Oxford: Clarendon Press, 1892).

II. WRITINGS ON HEGEL

A. Books

Bloch, Ernst. *Subjekt-Objekt: Erläuterungen zu Hegel*. 2nd ed. rev. (Frankfurt a/M: Suhrkamp Verlag, 1962).

Bodammer, Theodor, *Hegels Deutung der Sprache*, Interpretationen zu Hegels Äusserungen über die Sprache (Hamburg: F. Meiner, 1969).

Chapelle, A., *Hegel et la religion*, 3 vols. (Paris: Editions universitaires, 1964).

Croce, B., *What is Living and What is Dead in Hegel's Philosophy*, Translated by D. Ainslie (London: MacMillan, 1915).

Dilthey, W., *Die Jugendgeschichte Hegels*, vol. IX of his *Gesammelte Schriften* (Leipzig: B. H. Teubner, 1921).

Fackenheim, E., *The Religious Dimension in Hegel's Thought* (Bloomington, Ind.: Indiana University Press, 1967).

Fetscher, I., *Hegels Lehre von Menschen*. Kommentar zu den §§ 387-482 der *Enzyklopädie der Philosophischen Wissenschaften* (Stuttgart: F. Frommann, 1970).

Feuerbach, L., *Philosophische Kritiken und Grundsätze*, ed. F. Jodl, vol. II of his *Sämtliche Werke*, ed. W. Bolin and F. Jodl (Stuttgart: F. Frommann [E. Hauff], 1904).

Findlay, J. N., *Hegel: A Re-examination* (New York: Collier, 1962).

Gadamer, H.-G., *Hegels Dialektik: Fünf hermeneutische Studien* (Tübingen: J. C. B. Mohr [Paul Siebeck], 1971).

Glockner, H., *Die Voraussetzungen der Hegelschen Philosophie*, vol. I of *Hegel*. 3rd ed. rev. (Stuttgart: F. Fromman, 1934).

Hartmann, Nicolai, *Die Philosophie des Deutschen Idealismus*, (Berlin: de Gruyter, 1960).

Heidegger, Martin, *Holzwege* (Frankfurt am Main: V. Klosterman, 1963).

Hyppolite, Jean, *Logique et existence: Essai sur la Logique de Hegel* (Paris: Press Universitaires de France, 1961).

Kaufmann, Walter, *Hegel: Reinterpretation, Texts, and Commentary* (New York: Doubleday & Company, Inc., 1965).

Kimmerle, H., *Das Problem der Abgeschlossenheit des Denkens*. Hegels "System der Philosophie" in den Jahren 1800-1804, Supplement 8 of *Hegel Studien* (Bonn: Bouvier, 1970).

Kojève, Alexandre, *Introduction à la lecture de Hegel: Leçons sur la Phénoménologie de l'esprit, professées de 1933 à 1939...*, réunis et publiées par Raimond Queneau (Paris: Gallimard 1947).

Lauener, Henri, *Die Sprache in der Philosophie Hegels mit besonderer Berücksichtigung der Aesthetik* (Bern: P. Haupt, 1962).

Lowenberg, J., *Hegel's "Phenomenology": Dialogues on the Life of Mind* (La Salle, Illinois: Open Court, 1965).

Löwith, Karl, *From Hegel to Nietzsche* (New York: Holt, Rinehart & Winston, 1964).

Marcuse, Herbert, *Reason and Revolution: Hegel and the Rise of Social Theory* (Oxford: Oxford University Press, 1941).

Marx, W., *Absolute Reflexion und Sprache* (Frankfurt a/M: V. Klostermann, 1967).

Mure, G. R. G., *An Introduction to Hegel* (Oxford: Clarendon Press, 1940).

—, *A Study of Hegel's Logic* (Oxford: Clarendon Press, 1950).

—, *The Philosophy of Hegel* (London: Oxford University Press, 1965).

Nink, C., *Kommentar zu der grundlegenden Abschnitten von Hegels Phänomenologie* (Regensburg, 1931).

Purpus, Wilhelm, *Die Dialektick der sinnlichen Gewissheit bei Hegel* (Nürnberg, 1905).

Rosenkranz, Karl, *Georg Wilhelm Friedrich Hegels Leben* (Berlin: Duncker und Humblott, 1844).

Royce, J., *Lectures on Modern Idealism* (New Haven: Yale University Press, 1964).

Simon, J., *Das Problem der Sprache bei Hegel* (Köln: Photo-Stelle der Universitäts Köln, 1957).

Soll, I., *An Introduction to Hegel's Metaphysics* (Chicago: University of Chicago Press, 1969).

Wallace, William, *Prolegomena to the Study of Hegel's Philosophy and especially of his Logic* (Oxford: Oxford University Press, 1874).

B. *Articles and Reviews*

Andler, C., "Le fondement du savoir dans la Phénoménologie de l'Esprit", *Revue de Metaphysique et de Morale*, XXXVIII (July-September, 1931), 317-340.

Clark, M., "Meaning and Language in Hegel's Philosophy", *Revue Philosophique de Louvain*, 58 (1960), 557-578.

Copleston, F. C., "*Hegel and the Rationalisation of Mysticism*", *Talk of God* (Royal Institute of Philosophy, Vol. II) (London: MacMillan, 1967), 118-132.

Derbolav, J., "Hegel und die Sprache", *Sprache-Schlüssel zur Welt: Festschrift für Leo Weisgerber* (Düsseldorf: Pädagogischer Verlag Schwann, 1959), 56-86.

Fichte, J. G., "Von der Sprachfähigkeit und dem Ursprung der Sprache", *Philosophisches Journal, Einer Gesellschaft* Deutscher Gelehrten, I, 3, (1795), 255-273.

Habermas, J., "Arbeit und Interaktion: Bemerkungen zu Hegels Jenenser Philosophie des Geistes", *Natur und Geschichte: Karl Löwith zum 70. Geburtstag* (Stuttgart: Kohlhammer, 1967), 132-155.

Heidegger, Martin, "Hegels Begriff der Erfahrung", *Holzwege* (Frankfurt am Main: V. Klostermann, 1963), 105-192.

Honigswald, R., "Gedanken zur Philosophie Hegels", *Preussische Jahrbücher*, vol. 226, no. 2 (1931), 148-168.

Knox, T. M., A Review of G. M. G. Mure's *A Study of Hegel's Logic* in *Philosophy*, XXVI, 97 (1951), 180-183.

Koyré, Alexandre, "Note sur la langue et la terminologie hégéliennes", *Revue Philosophique de la France et de l'Etranger*, CXII (1931), 406-439.

Lowenberg, "The Comedy of Immediacy in Hegel's 'Phenomenology'", *Mind*, XLIV (1935), 21-38.

Pöggeler, O., "Hegel, der Verfasser des Ältesten Systemprogram des Deutschen Idealismus", Supplement 4 to *Hegel-Studien* (1969), 18-32.

Rosenzweig, F., "Das älteste Systemprogramm des deutschen Idealismus: Ein handschriftlicher Fund", *Sitzungsberichte der Heidelberger Akademie der Wissenschaften: Philosophisch-historische Klasse*, VIII (1917), 1-50.

Royce, Josiah, "Hegel's Terminology". *Dictionary of Philosophy and Psychology*, (ed.) J. M. Baldwin (New York: Peter Smith, 1940), I, 454-465.

Simon, J., "Die Kategorien im 'gewöhnlichen' und im 'spekulativen' Satz:

Bemerkungen zu Hegels Wissenschaftsbegriff", *Wiener Jahrbuch für Philosophie*, III (1970), 9-37.

Teyssèdre, B., "Hegel à Stuttgart", *Revue philosophique de la France et de l'Etranger*, CL (1960), 2, 197-227.

Wahl, J., "Hegel et Heidegger", *La pensée de Hegel*, by A. Marietti (Paris: Bordas, 1957), 185-95.

Walsh, W. H., "On the Philosophy of Hegel", *Philosophy*, XXVII (1953), 207-228.

III. OTHER WORKS

Cassirer, Ernst, *The Philosophy of Symbolic Forms*, tr. R. Manheim, 3 vols. (New Haven: Yale University Press, 1953).

Fiesel, E., *Die Sprachphilosophie der Deutschen Romantik* (Tübingen: J. C. B. Mohr [Paul Siebeck], 1927).

Heintel, E. (ed.), *J. G. Herder: Sprachphilosophische Schriften* (Hamburg: F. Meiner, 1960).

Herder, J. G. "Essay on the Origin of Language", tr. A. Gode, *On the Origin of Language*, (New York: F. Unger, 1966).

Leibniz, G. W., *Muttersprache und völkische Gesinnung*, vol. I of his *Deutsche Schriften*, ed. W. Schmied-Kowarzik (Leipzig: F. Meiner, 1916).

Lessing, G. E., *Emilia Galotti*, Trans. Edward Dvoretzky (New York: Frederick Unger, 1962).

Urban, W. M., *Language and Reality. The Philosophy of Language and The Principles of Symbolism* (New York: Macmillan, 1951).

INDEX

JANUA LINGUARUM

STUDIA MEMORIAE NICOLAI VAN WIJK DEDICATA
Edited by C. H. van Schooneveld
SERIES MINOR

67. ROBERT L. MILLER: The Linguistic Relativity Principle and New Humboldtian Ethnolinguistics: A History and Appraisal. 1968. 127 pp.   Gld. 20.—

69. I. M. SCHLESINGER: Sentence Structure and the Reading Process. 1968. 172 pp.   Gld. 22.—

70. A. ORTIZ and E. ZIERER: Set Theory and Linguistics. 1968. 64 pp.   Gld. 12.—

71. HANS-HEINRICH LIEB: Communication Complexes and Their Stages. 1968. 140 pp.   Gld. 20.—

72. ROMAN JAKOBSON: Child Language, Aphasia and Phonological Universals. 1968. 104 pp.   Gld. 12.—

73. CHARLES F. HOCKETT: The State of the Art. 1968. 124 pp.   Gld. 18.—

74. A. JUILLAND and HANS-HEINRICH LIEB: "Klasse" und "Klassifikation" in der Sprachwissenschaft. 1968. 75 pp.   Gld. 14.—

76. URSULA OOMEN: Automatische Syntaktische Analyse. 1968. 84 pp.   Gld. 16.—

77. ALDO D. SCAGLIONE: Ars Grammatica. 1970. 151 pp.   Gld. 18.—

106. HENRIK BIRNBAUM: Problems of Typological and Genetic Linguistics Viewed in a Generative Framework. 1971. 132 pp.   Gld. 16.—

107. NOAM CHOMSKY: Studies on Semantics in Generative Grammar. 1972. 207 pp.   Gld. 24.—

110. MANFRED BIERWISCH: Modern Linguistics. Its Development, Methods and Problems. 1971. 105 pp.   Gld. 12.—

113. ERHARD AGRICOLA: Semantische Relationen im Text und im System. 1972. 127 pp.   Gld. 26.—

114. ROMAN JAKOBSON: Studies on Child Language and Aphasia. 1971. 132 pp.   Gld. 16.—

117. D. L. OLMSTED: Out of the Mouth of Babes. 1971. 260 pp. Gld. 36.—

119. HERMAN PARRET: Language and Discourse. 1971. 292 pp. Gld. 32.—

123. JOHN W. OLLER: Coding Information in Natural Languages. 1971. 120 pp.   Gld. 20.—

134. ROMAN JAKOBSON: A Bibliography of His Writings. With a Foreword by C. H. Van Schooneveld. 1971. 60 pp.   Gld. 10.—

MOUTON · PUBLISHERS · THE HAGUE